How to Survive

WORRY

How to Handle
WORRY

A Catholic Approach

Marshall J. Cook

Pauline
BOOKS & MEDIA
Boston

Library of Congress Cataloging-in-Publication Data

Cook, Marshall, 1944–
    How to handle worry : a Catholic approach / Marshall Cook.
        p. cm.
    Includes bibliographical references.
    ISBN 0-8198-3390-8 (pbk.)
    1. Christian life—Catholic authors. 2. Worry—Religious aspects—Catholic Church.
    3. Peace of mind—Religious aspects—Catholic Church. I. Title.
    BX2350.3.C664 2007
    248.8'6—dc22

                                    2007007589

The Scripture quotations contained herein are from the *New Revised Standard Version Bible: Catholic Edition*, copyright © 1989, 1993, Division of Christian Education of the National Council of the Churches of Christ in the United States of America. Used by permission. All rights reserved.

Cover design by Rosana Usselmann

Cover photo © istockphoto.com/Peter Zelei

"P" and PAULINE are registered trademarks of the Daughters of St. Paul.

Published by Pauline Books & Media, 50 Saint Paul's Avenue, Boston, MA 02130-3491. www.pauline.org.

Printed in the U.S.A.

Pauline Books & Media is the publishing house of the Daughters of St. Paul, an international congregation of women religious serving the Church with the communications media.

1 2 3 4 5 6 7 8 9   12 11 10 09 08 07

Contents

Preface: A Brief Note about Your Author, an "Expert" on Worry

I've taught for the University of Wisconsin-Madison for twenty-five years, and I speak at seminars and conferences all across the country. I've published several books on stress management and even been a guest on Oprah to discuss the topic.

When I approach the podium in some faraway city, clutching my handouts and notes, the moderator introduces me as an "expert." Folks look to me for answers. They honor me by spending their precious time listening to me. So I'd better be an expert.

But I'm no Ted Williams expert. I'm a Charlie Lau expert.

Ted Williams hit .344 over nineteen seasons in major league baseball, which is way better than good. He hit 521 home runs, also an extraordinary mark. In 1941 he batted .406, making him the last player to hit over .400 for a full season. Williams was surely an expert on hitting; he could do it better than anyone who ever lived.

That's not the kind of expert I am.

Charlie Lau batted just .255 over eleven seasons in the majors and hit just sixteen home runs. And yet, perhaps because he worked so hard and thought so much about hitting, Lau became an outstanding hitting instructor. Whenever he set out to teach a team to hit better, the team hit better. He had a system, and he worked hard to explain it effectively, so others could put it to good use.

If I'm any kind of an expert, I'm a Charlie Lau kind of expert. I know how to identify and deal with anxiety. I *know* worry, and I'm learning each day how to let faith defeat fear.

Writing is a tool of discovery for me. This will be our mutual exploration as we learn to confront and overcome our fears. Our fears are different; our strategies will be different. But we will share the journey.

"We know that all things work for good for those who love God, who are called according to his purpose" (Rom 8:28).

Introduction

A great deal has happened in our world in the eight years since I first wrote *How to Handle Worry: A Catholic Approach* (Pauline Books & Media, 1999). Much of it is bad news.

We now live in the "post-9/11" world. Since that fatal and tragic day in 2001, Americans have been aware of how vulnerable we really are.

We live in a perpetual state of tension, fighting a "war on terrorism" against an enemy none can see and few can understand. We even have a color-coded system of alerts to let us know how scared we should be at any given time.

The slaughter of innocents on our own soil in 2001 wasn't the only traumatic event of the last seven years. To the "normal" natural disasters of earthquake and storm, fire, flood, and famine, add the horrific hurricane that at least temporarily destroyed a major American city, and a tsunami that wiped away whole towns and thousands of lives.

I've had my share of private tsunamis to deal with as well— as I suspect you have, too. Emergency surgery brought me closely in touch with my own mortality. I've grieved the deaths of friends and mourned the passing of more of the heroes of my youth. My wife Ellen and I are still mourning the recent death of her mother.

It's a frightening and difficult world we live in.

But surely it was ever thus. Is the world really a more fearsome place now than before?

When I was growing up in Altadena—a peaceful small town in the shadow of the San Gabriel Mountains of southern California—I found school to be a terrifying place. Along with the three R's, I encountered the three T's: teasing, taunting, and tests of courage. You probably did, too.

The children of my day also experienced the dawning of the nuclear age. Without warning, our teacher would yell, "Drop!" and we would immediately scramble under our desks, bumping heads and scraping knees. There we huddled, arms over our heads, until given the all-clear.

How those rickety wooden desks were supposed to protect us from a nuclear bomb I've never quite understood, and apparently I didn't really believe it even then; my nightmares were frequently haunted by mushroom clouds.

I reached puberty—surely terrifying enough in any environment—about the same time the Russians launched *Sputnik*. The Soviets had beaten us into space, rendering us vulnerable to all sorts of previously undreamed of attacks. For me this did not mean more drop drills but an increase in the amount of math and science I was expected to learn. And some of those courses made me want to duck under my desk and cover my head.

Soviet Premier Nikita Khrushchev took off his shoe and pounded it on his desk at the United Nations, vowing to bury me and my fellow Americans. Missiles bearing nuclear warheads sprouted on Cuban soil, just ninety miles from our shores. The news brought pictures of black people being assaulted with fire hoses, threatened with dogs, and beaten with clubs—not in some faraway country but in the America I pledged allegiance to at school every morning.

As I got older, I protested America's involvement in the Vietnam War, facing the threat of imprisonment or immigration from the country I love. My heroes—John F. Kennedy, his brother Robert, and Martin Luther King, Jr.——were cut down by assassins' bullets. Their deaths devastated me. Chaos seemed to rule the earth.

And perhaps it does.

The end of the world is near — again

As the World Trade Towers fell, and the images flashed across our TV screens again and again, some people might have thought they were witnessing the beginning of the end—not just of the United States but of the world itself.

Others had expected the end to come with the new millennium and the "Y2K disaster" that would surely wipe out our collective computer consciousness and destroy civilization.

Actually, the end of the world seems to have been postponed dozens, even hundreds, of times. Predictions of the world's certain demise circulated widely in 1844 and again in 1914. More recently, groups like the Heaven's Gate cult have given horrific testimony to the strength and compelling nature of such predictions. Today the "Left Behind" novels, which describe end times, enjoy enormous popularity.

The Jehovah's Witnesses have been wrong so often in trying to pin a number to Armageddon, they've quit trying. A spokesman for the denomination, Robert Johnson, has said, "We learned our lesson.... The Bible has a list of about two dozen things to watch out for. They've all happened."[1] As J. Gordon Melton, head of the Institute for the Study of American Religion, points out: "Everyone who predicted the end of the world had one thing in common. They were wrong."[2]

---

1. John Dart, "Jehovah's Witnesses Abandon End-of-the-World Prediction" (Religion News Service, December 1, 1995).

2. Ibid.

If unwilling to put a specific date to it, many Christians still believe that the end time prophesized in the Book of Revelation is imminent.

How will it come when it comes? Perhaps dirty radioactive bombs or the accidental release of nuclear weapons will do us in. Some say it will be the fire of global warming, while others favor a new ice age. Pollution? A bacterial infection or virus? All seem like worthy candidates for the role of Earth's executioner.

If the world doesn't go out with a bang, one day it will most certainly go out with a whimper. The sun that sustains all life on earth won't last forever, after all; scientists predict that it will burn itself out in a mere five billion years, give or take a hundred million.

At least nobody seems to be too worried about that one yet.

How we hope to cope— and why it isn't working

In the face of all this disaster—real, imagined, and prophesized—we've typically reacted as a culture by evading, avoiding, and denying.

We dull the senses with alcohol, marijuana, cocaine, food, and television, losing ourselves in endless, often mindless activity.

We treat aging as a disease, which many seem convinced is curable. We pursue eternal youth through chemical injections of poison to fill out wrinkles, liposuction to suck out fat, supplements to boost our energy, and drugs to keep us virile.

We have become gripped by a psychology of scarcity. There isn't enough for everyone—enough money, enough possessions, enough time; better grab as much for yourself as you can while the grabbing's good. This mentality is never more obvious than at the approach of the "holiday season," which now seems to begin shortly after the Fall Equinox. "Got your shopping done yet?" folks start asking around Labor Day, and the day after Thanksgiving becomes a mass mall free-for-all, "the busiest shopping day of the year."

Has "Make hay while the sun shines" replaced "In God we trust" as our national credo?

The paradox of the faith filled, fearful Christian

The Bible tells us that the world is not our home and that it will one day pass away. But it also tells us we don't know when that's going to happen.

And even if we did, why should we as believers worry about it? We say we believe in a loving Father-God who will send his Son to gather us, living and dead, at the end of time and bring us home.

Don't we want that? Do we really even believe it? Why do we let anxiety rule us even in the presence of our faith?

While I was growing up fearful, I was also growing up Christian. I went to church every Sunday, prayed with fervor, and felt God's daily presence in my life. As a young adult I converted to Catholicism, the faith of my father's people and of my heart, reaffirming my belief in a loving God who gave us his only-begotten Son that we might have life in abundance for eternity in his presence.

I believed then, and I believe now, that Jesus Christ is the living Son of the living God, and that his death on the cross redeemed me and won for me my salvation.

And yet for years fear and faith coexisted in me, with fear often gaining the upper hand. Only in recent years has faith finally come to dominate—although not yet fully banish—fear.

How could this be?

More importantly, if you, too, have struggled with your dual nature as a faith-filled, fearful Catholic, how can you allow healing to occur in your soul, so that your faith can finally triumph?

That question propels this book into being. In these pages, we'll seek the path that leads away from anxiety and toward the peace that surpasses all earthly understanding.

Guided by the Word, we will name and face our fears, opening our hearts to God's healing love. When we do, we will learn to live more fully in faith, freed at last from needless anxiety.

CHAPTER 1

Bringing Our Burdens to God

At the chapel where I attend daily Mass, Father Victor from nearby Milwaukee often pinch-hits when Father Randy has to be elsewhere. Speaking in a thick Italian accent, Father Victor always begins the celebration of Eucharist by thanking God for calling us together for "the great gift of the Mass."

Oh, but sometimes we don't seem very enthusiastic about that gift!

As Catholics most of us believe that we are obligated to attend Mass on Sundays and on occasional other "Holy Days of Obligation." And that's how a lot of us act when we get there—as if we're there under duress, because we're obligated. We mumble our way through the responses, sink into a near coma or drift off into space during the homily, and stare vacantly during the hymn singing. We start struggling into our coats—if we even bothered to take them off in the first place—before the final blessing.

How differently we might behave if we thought of it as a Holy Day of Opportunity instead.

"If we really believed what we say we believe," I once heard a radio evangelist say, "they couldn't keep us away from church with shotguns. Why, we'd have to wear helmets and shoulder pads, because we'd be bouncing off the walls with excitement and joy." We'd even be willing to die for the faith—as martyrs have done from the beginning of Christianity.

No, we don't have to start behaving like holy rollers, jumping up and running around the church every time the Spirit strikes us. But shouldn't we be showing more enthusiasm for the great gift of the Eucharist and the solace and support that come from communal worship?

If we really think about it, rule or no rule, don't we go to Mass, at least on some level, because we want and need to?

"Not my brother or my sister, but it's me, O Lord," so the old song goes, "standing in the need of prayer."

At each Mass we recite the prayer that Jesus himself gave us, the one we call the Lord's Prayer. We pause while the priest petitions the Father on our behalf to deliver us from every evil, to grant us peace in our day, to free us from all sin, and to protect us from all anxiety "as we wait in joyful hope for the coming of our Savior, Jesus Christ."

We affirm this prayer with a communal "Amen": we believe!

But do we? Do we *really* believe that God will keep his promise to grant us his peace and free us from every fear?

Granted, our belief is imperfect, our faith incomplete. The cry of the father whose child had an unclean spirit is our cry, too: "I believe; help my unbelief!" (Mk 9:24). But shouldn't even an imperfect faith in God's perfect love protect us from the corrosive anxiety that can rob life of its joy?

"Do not fear, only believe," Jesus tells the ruler of the synagogue, whose daughter has just died (Mk 5:36). We are to have absolute faith in the saving power of Jesus, even in the face of death.

Can the truth really be that simple? It can and it is, but that doesn't mean it's easy. Somehow the simplest truths are the most elusive.

If we truly bring our worries and fears to God, allowing him to release us from our anxiety so that we may more fully love him, we will be acting contrary to our cultural teaching and example. Pessimism and cynicism are considered "natural" and "realistic," while the optimist is labeled a "Pollyanna," out of touch with the cold, hard facts of life.

It isn't true. The Word of Christ is true.

In the chapters that follow, we'll look at ways our culture fosters and nurtures our fears and explore Christ's teachings about anxiety and our reactions to his clear, simple truth. We'll discover together how to let him take away all our fears. We'll explore worry and stress as a universal part of the human condition. We'll examine the difference between useful worry—the kind that helps us to avoid danger, prepare for challenges, and solve problems—and the senseless anxiety that paralyzes us by robbing us of energy and will while it eats away at our faith.

We'll trace worry to its roots, learn why we cling to certain worries, and come to understand that the behaviors we adopt to ease the pain of anxiety often in fact intensify our fears and perpetuate our anxiety.

Since worry often becomes automatic, the expected response, it can feel like a natural instinct, which is to say it doesn't "feel" at all, and we aren't even aware of it. We'll learn to catch ourselves in the act of worrying, so we can choose another alternative.

We'll explore the limits of positive thinking, making sure we're seeing life as it is, not as we would like it to be. And we'll confront our anxiety rather than evade it. We'll name our demons, giving them tangible shape and substance; then we'll let Christ expel them from us.

We'll even delineate different types and sources of worry, because they may require different responses. (Like the evil spirits Christ banishes in the New Testament, worries are legion.)

With dear, good Martha, we'll learn at times to put aside our chores to live wholly in the moment, in communion with our Lord. We'll stop "sweating the small stuff"—and give all the "large stuff" to God.

We'll even practice the gentle art of accepting the inevitable and letting go of the past. We'll renounce revenge in favor of forgiveness, following the higher road Christ invites us to walk with him. It's not enough, after all, to simply refrain from killing our brother or sister. We are to banish the killing impulse from our hearts—and with it the horrendous anxiety it produces in us.

Christ can heal us of all anxiety if we but let him. When we do, we'll re-encounter the central paradox of our faith, the teaching that we must willingly lose our lives in order to find full and abundant Life in him. We find freedom from fear in surrendering to God's will and accepting God's amazing promises for us, manifested in his Word and made flesh in his Son.

"Surrender" sounds so easy, but we know it to be so hard. This journey will require time, concentration, and energy.

Are you ready to start?

The path from faith to fear is the journey of a lifetime. We must pick ourselves—and each other—up every time we fall. We must forgive every time we fail.

We'll never be finished or "cured" as long as we live on this earth. We'll continue to confront fears every day of our lives, and every day our faith will become stronger and anxiety will lose a bit more of its hold on us.

"Don't be afraid; just have faith." The truth really is that simple. But it defies intuition and emotion and transcends intellect and logic. It won't be enough to learn about the journey; we must live it.

> *"Often I am like a small boat on the ocean,*
> *completely at the mercy of the waves."*
>
> — HENRI NOUWEN

CHAPTER 2

Why Worry Is Inevitable

Early in his public ministry, Jesus cast off from shore in a small boat with his disciples. A violent storm came up without warning, threatening to swamp the boat and terrifying its occupants.

Or all but one of them, anyway. Jesus was sleeping soundly.

"Lord, save us! We are perishing!" the disciples exhorted him.

"Where is your courage?" he replied. "How little faith you have."

Then the Savior stood up, Matthew reports, "and rebuked the winds and the sea; and there was a dead calm."

"What sort of man is this," they said, "that even the winds and the sea obey him?" (cf. Mt 8:23–27)

Hadn't they been paying attention when, earlier that day, he had cured Peter's mother-in-law of her fever by simply taking her by the hand? Weren't they watching when, later that evening, he expelled many unclean spirits by a simple command?

They were still new to discipleship, and it must have been hard for them to believe what they were seeing and hearing from this Jesus.

But even after seeing him feed five thousand with a few loaves and fishes, they succumbed to fear amid stormy waters. After the miraculous multiplication, Jesus "made the disciples get into the boat and go on ahead to the other side," Matthew tells us (14:22), "while he dismissed the crowds." Then Jesus went up the mountain to pray.

Later, several hundred yards from shore, the boat encountered strong head winds. When the disciples saw Jesus walking toward them on the water, they became more frightened of him than of the storm, believing him to be a ghost.

"Take heart," he told them, "it is I; do not be afraid" (Mt 14:27).

Impetuous Peter demanded proof, so the Lord bade him to walk out on the water himself. And he did it—at least for as long as he kept his eye on Jesus. But the moment Peter looked away at the fearsome waves, he began to sink.

"You of little faith, why did you doubt?" Jesus chided him.

When Jesus again calmed the winds, the disciples knew that "truly you are the Son of God" (cf. Mt 14:28–33).

Well, they knew for the moment, anyway. Like us, they would falter again and again, letting fear overcome faith. Even in the presence of the Master, they were often unable to escape their anxieties.

Although our stormy seas are mostly metaphorical, we, like the first disciples, often feel at the mercy of the tempest.

To seek a perfect world

What would a truly carefree life look like? It's almost impossible to imagine, isn't it? Could we really strip away all those things that provoke anxiety in us? And if we did, what would be left?

Forty years ago, two social scientists tried to assign numbers to various stress-inducing events in life. They allotted ninety-nine "stress points" to experiencing the death of a spouse, number one on their list. Not far behind, with ninety-one points, was divorce. Other high stressors included being fired and going to jail. No surprises there.

But the number-three stressor on the scale, weighing in at eighty-five points, might surprise you: marriage! Pregnancy also ranked high, with seventy-eight. (Note that the scale didn't specify unwanted marriage or pregnancy.) And here's a real shocker: number eleven on the list, at sixty-eight points, was retirement, followed five slots down by Christmas at fifty-six! Vacation also made the list, with forty-three points.

Wait a minute! These are good things, aren't they?

Good, yes. Stress-free, no.

When you go on that "carefree" vacation, for example, you leave behind your known world of routines and patterns, and you take on new roles like trail guide, scout, and tour director. Retirement confronts you with the challenge of redefining who you are and how to assign worth to your life. Christmas piles on a number of additional obligations without lessening the day-to-day struggles.

And all three require that you be happy. It's expected of you; anything short of complete harmony and bliss is failure.

"Personal achievement" is stressful (thirty-eight points' worth, according to the chart). Divorce, marriage, separation, and reconciliation are all stressful. A son or daughter leaving home provokes anxiety, but so does that same offspring moving back in.

The word "change" keeps appearing on the list: change of financial status (up or down); change of job or residence;

change in eating, sleeping, or exercise patterns—which means that any self-improvement program you undertake is likely to produce anxiety.

Another sociologist, Georgia Witkin, updated the scale in 1991 to include such previously unlisted stressors as raising a disabled child, single parenting, and infertility. "Husband's retirement" also made Witkin's list ("I married him for better or for worse," the old saying goes, "but not for lunch!"), as did "singlehood."

Being around people creates stress, but so does living alone.

Stress, then, is inevitable.

And that's not necessarily bad.

Even Christ worried

Scripture teaches that Jesus was "like us in all things save sin." Does that mean that, like us, even Jesus worried? Unless worry is a sin, he must have.

When life overwhelmed him, he withdrew from the crowds and went off by himself to pray—a stress reduction technique we'll revisit often in this little guide. He wept at the news of the death of his friend Lazarus. He literally sweated blood in the garden the night of his betrayal. He cried out to a God who had "forsaken" him on the cross.

Clearly, when Jesus came down from heaven to share our earthly existence, he experienced anxiety. And, as in all other aspects of life, he proved to be our best role model for handling stress.

If we can't escape the inevitable stressors of life, we'd better learn to handle the stress they produce in us. To do that, we need to understand what sorts of things worry us the most.

Numbers on a scale may help us gain some insight into stress, but they don't tell us much about our own individual responses. Just as we have different thresholds of pain, a different tolerance or even need for solitude, and different sleep requirements, so we are different in our perception of and ability to tolerate stress.

In addition, we react to experiences quite differently. A round of golf may be the ultimate relaxation for some but total aggravation for others. Some look forward all week to a nice social get-together on Friday night and the chance to meet new folks. For others, such a gathering is agony; they'd much rather work late.

As a beginning step in handling the inevitable anxiety in your life, consider keeping a worry-log for a few weeks. You can set aside a specific notebook or journal for this, or you can use *The Worry Workbook,* developed to accompany this text. Either way, the idea is to note the events of each day and the amount of anxiety they seem to produce in you.

If you keep track of your anxieties, you're likely to gain two benefits almost immediately.

Number one, you'll become more aware of your stress responses. This in turn will help you to know when to employ the stress-reducing techniques we'll discuss later. Eventually, you may even be able to cut off certain stresses before they occur!

Number two, you may be surprised about your reactions to life. Simply getting out of bed and getting ready for work in the morning may be an extremely stressful part of your day (especially during the winter in a harsh climate). That Friday night party, instead of being a reward, may be a tough challenge to your well-being. Washing dishes in steaming hot, soapy water may be for you as relaxing as a visit to a spa.

Why not find out? As you do so, read on to discover how your mind and body are reacting to all that stress.

> *"I'm dreaming of a white Christmas,*
> *just like the ones I used to know."*
>
> — IRVING BERLIN

CHAPTER 3

Christmas Comes but Once a Year —Thank God!

Maybe Scrooge wasn't entirely wrong in proclaiming Christmas to be a humbug.

"Hark the Herald Tribune sings, / advertising wondrous things," satirist Tom Lehrer sang. "God rest ye merry merchants, may / you make the yuletide pay."[1]

Well before the beginning of Advent—the holy liturgical season of prayer, reflection, and quiet anticipation of the coming of our Savior—the Christmas shopping season begins. Decorations, department store Santas, and Christmas sales start around Halloween now, and the day after Thanksgiving has become an unholy day of obligation, a national shopping day, with folks lining up before dawn to get first crack at huge "Black Friday" discounts. The race to consume has officially begun.

---

1. Tom Lehrer, "A Christmas Carol," from *An Evening Wasted with Tom Lehrer* (Lehrer Records, released March 1959).

It has clearly become our obligation as Americans to "boost retail sales" in this make-or-break season for purveyors of fruit-cakes, men's cologne, coffee table books, and other trifles we never buy except to give to someone else.

The television Christmas specials begin early, too; how else will they fit them all in before the big day? It's a Charlie Brown Christmas, and Rudolph the Red-Nosed Reindeer rides again —and again and again!

Where's the Grinch when we really need him?

By the second week of December, hucksters are urging us to finish our "last-minute shopping" as supplies of the season's hot items—including the year's fad toy—begin to dwindle. "Hurry! Supplies are limited. Get yours while they last."

Got your cards all sent? Christmas cookies baked? Packages wrapped and mailed? Better HURRY!

What do you buy for the guy in the next cubicle at work or for your second cousin twice removed—whom you neither really know nor particularly like? You have to get them some-thing; what if they get *you* something?

The eggnog begins to flow at office parties, house parties, and neighborhood parties, all leading up to the dreaded gather-ing of the clan. Over the turnpike and through airport securi-ty, to grandmother's condo in Florida we go for the traditional overeating and swapping of loot.

No time to go to church? Not to worry. Last year, some evangelical churches actually cancelled Christmas services, a development that still stuns me into befuddled silence when I think of it.

All too soon it's time to bundle up the exhausted, sated chil-dren and head for home—and the quick build-up to New Year's Eve, the night when amateur drunks turn the roads into a demolition derby, and we feel compelled to make New Year's resolutions we know we'll never keep.

January 1 ushers in not only the New Year but also the Season of the Great Letdown. The morning newspaper brings advice on hangover remedies and diets "to shed those unwanted holiday pounds" we were all required to pack on. The paper bulges with advertising inserts for post-holiday sales, including half off on all Christmas items.

Garbage cans overflow with wrapping paper, boxes, and broken toys, and the carcasses of Yule trees litter the curbsides. Instead of catalogs, the mail now brings a tidal wave of credit card bills. Instead of silver bells, you hear the sound of interest rates and late fees piling up.

The good times are over; the long winter is upon us. There's nothing to look forward to, no holiday to anticipate until Valentine's Day.

Almost lost is the fact that, for the Christian, December 25 doesn't end the liturgical season; it begins it!

An overly cynical view of our most beloved holiday? I hope so—and fear not. But regardless of what you think about the Christmas we observe in our society, it has become for most of us not a time of peace and prayer but of intense stress.

Just why is Christmas so stressful?

For openers, most of us virtually double our work loads during the pre-Christmas build-up. Work and family obligations don't stop while we're shopping, partying, and planning. Preparation for Christmas comes in addition to, not instead of, everything else. True, some industries pretty much grind to a halt in December, but most of us don't work in those industries. Offices keep right on running, the garbage still needs collecting, the mail—a staggering flood of it—still needs delivering, and sales clerks work longer hours and deal with more frantic and surly people than at any other time of the year.

Our culture doesn't simply demand that we observe Christmas, with all the glittery trimmings. We must experience joy while we do it! Poignant ads for coffee and beer paint portraits of stirring reunions with loved ones and treks into the country for an old-fashioned Yule, where we are enveloped in the warmth of family and hearthside.

But reality for most of us doesn't measure up to the Hallmark Card version. Those who are alone feel even lonelier at Christmas. Those from "dysfunctional families" (is there any other kind?) become more acutely aware of strained relations with their relations. Regrets become more powerful.

Many carry memories of past Christmases as a sort of Paradise Lost, a time of innocence when they still believed in Santa Claus (and Jesus?), or at least their kids did.

It's hard to keep Christmas in your heart when that heart is aching.

And then, of course, there are the millions of non-Christians—Muslims, Jews, Buddhists, agnostics, and atheists—for whom Christmas is a loud distraction at best, a constant reminder of their minority status at worst.

The suicide myth

Conventional wisdom tells us that the suicide rate spikes during the Christmas season. I believed that for years—until I actually looked up the statistics as I prepared to write this chapter.

Turns out, like so many truisms, that this one isn't true at all.

According to every reliable source I've checked, although rates of depression go up, suicide rates actually decrease slightly at this time of year. July and August, not December and January, have the highest rates of suicide.

That's not to say that suicide isn't a constant reality in our culture and our world. According to statistics from the year 2000, someone somewhere on the planet commits suicide every forty seconds. That's a total of 815,000 persons a year (well over double the number who have died in armed conflict). Vulnerable teenagers are especially at risk when they go back to school in the fall. And men are four times more likely than women to succeed in taking their own lives.

If Christmas is so stressful and, for many, excruciatingly painful, why doesn't the suicide rate rise during that season? I have a hunch. Even if family relationships are strained, we are at least trying to nurture them at this season. We perform acts of charity, however small. Even if the present is hastily bought and not especially well received, gift-giving affirms the giver and the receiver.

Most importantly, even though we seem to be doing our best to try to obscure if not extinguish the true meaning of Christmas, our celebration of the incarnation of God has tremendous power. Whether we take the time to consciously acknowledge it or not, Christians are proclaiming the Word, singing the sacred songs, and reading the holy texts. Even those who call Christmas a "humbug" can't change its true nature.

What to do about the "problem of Christmas"

I believe that the two true enemies of Christmas are noise and clutter. Thus I believe the "solution" to Christmas stress lies in reducing both.

Advent should be a time of inner quiet as we wait in joyful hope for the coming of our Lord Jesus—coming to be born at Bethlehem, coming into hearts prepared to receive him, and coming again in his glory at the end of time. We can often find our God only in the still, small voice. We must create periods of quiet and calm in the midst of the chaos of Christmas. Try setting aside special prayer time to listen for that voice. Read and reflect on the Scriptures. Take a break from Christmas frenzy at least once a day to celebrate Christmas peace.

When those chirpy voices on the television and radio start berating you on the day after Thanksgiving to get to that "last-minute" Christmas shopping—and to spend more money than you can afford!—muster your firm resolve to tune them out!

Plan to do less this Christmas. Cut back on card and gift lists a bit, pass on some of the secular activities that don't connect with the meaning of the season, and let someone else have the big family party this year. (Someone may be waiting to be asked.) Are you sure you need to bake thirty-six batches of Christmas cookies?

Eliminate rituals and customs that no longer sustain you— if indeed they ever did—and consider creating new ones that serve you better. Build your Christmas around personal and communal worship.

You won't change society. The madness will continue unabated. But you'll be keeping Christmas in your heart, which is where it has always belonged, and you will be spreading the peace of Christ to those you love.

"Worry never robs tomorrow of its sorrow;
it only saps today of its joy."

— LEO BUSCAGLIA

CHAPTER 4

Why Worry Hurts Us

"Worrying about it won't help."

We all know the truth of this adage, and we all go right on worrying anyway.

Worry wastes your time and energy. It disrupts your rest, hurts your ability to make decisions, and robs you of the pleasure and satisfaction you should get from work and play.

When you worry, you don't plan; you obsess, imagining the worst. You ignore the present to fret over a future that never comes. You reject the sweet gift of now to chase the chimera of then.

Worrying is like paying interest on a debt. You have nothing to show for it, you still have to pay back the principal, and you have no money left for the things you really need. Substitute energy and enthusiasm for money and you understand why worry hurts you.

A researcher named Hans Selye can help you understand just how much.

Selye was a pioneer in stress research and probably the first scientist to use the word "stress" the way we're using it here, to mean the internal physical and physiological responses to outside stressors.

In one famous experiment, Selye put mice into a refrigerator to see how they would react to the stress of numbing but not lethal cold. (My wife and son and I conducted the same experiment on ourselves when we moved from California to Wisconsin years ago.)

Selye made sure to provide the mice with all the necessities of life, including the company of other mice. The only real change was the temperature.

Invariably the mice reacted in three distinct stages. First they hunkered down and sulked. (They seemed to sulk, anyway. It's hard to tell when a mouse is depressed.) But in stage two, they got busy building nests, discovering their food sources, and acting cooperatively to cope with their challenging environment.

So far, so good. But then their activity became frenetic. After a period of intense activity, the over-stressed mice invariably died.

Selye concluded that stress had literally killed them, and he theorized that it could kill us in the same way. Scientists use mice in their experiments, after all, because rodent systems tend to react in much the same ways as our systems do. High levels of prolonged stress suppress our immune systems, leaving us open to disease. The famous "fight or flight" reflex in response to perceived danger creates a rush of corticoids in our system. These chemicals act as abrasives, scratching the insides of our artery walls. The body repairs the damage with plaque. Given enough stress, the build-up of plaque can constrict the blood flow through the arteries, leading to heart disease and strokes. If you live in a continual state of semipanic, maintaining a high baseline level of stress, it will take a horrible physical toll—not to mention the damage it does to your spirit and your psyche.

But just as too much stress hurts you, so also does too little stress. Selye concluded from this and other experiments that the lack of stressors could promote lethargy, boredom, even depression. You experience an appropriate, manageable level of stress as stimulation and challenge. If you aren't being challenged, you may feel useless, and so life lacks purpose and meaning.

So Selye coined the term "eustress"—not too much, not too little, but just the right amount of stress (challenge) to keep you happily productive while allowing you enough rest and recreation to live a healthy, balanced life.

How much stress is just enough to create eustress differs for each of us. You need to learn to find and maintain your own ideal stress level, so that when disaster does strike and stress spikes, you can handle it until life gentles again.

Consider my friend and colleague, Miranda. Like me, she moved with her family from California to Wisconsin and now works in the Department of Liberal Studies and the Arts at the University in Madison. Her life is quite full—a demanding job, a husband, and two rambunctious little boys to raise, plus the challenge of relocating to the new climate and culture of the great upper Midwest.

But apparently that wasn't enough challenge for Miranda. She auditioned for and landed the lead role as Martha in a local production of Edward Albee's *Who's Afraid of Virginia Woolf?* This play is a workout just to watch, let alone to perform! And yet, Miranda was able to sprint up and down the emotional scales five nights a week and twice on Saturdays—while still keeping up with job and family!

Her reaction?

"It was such fun! I loved it."

The stress might have killed me, but Miranda was in her eustress zone and did just fine.

How to tell "good worry" from "bad worry"

Each new generation imagines that it invented stress and has more to be anxious about than its parents did, but this is not so. Worry has always been with us.

"To live is to worry," Dr. C. W. Saleeby wrote in 1907. "The cause of worry is life; its cure is death."[1] Worry stems from our desire to live and to be happy, Saleeby noted. If we care about outcomes, we worry. Worry has been common to all races in all times, a natural state of conscious living.

"To venture causes anxiety," philosopher Søren Kierkegaard noted over a century ago, "but not to venture is to lose oneself."[2] He called anxiety "our best teacher" and linked it to the freedom to choose among possibilities. Anxiety, he wrote, is "the dizziness of freedom.... He who has learned rightly to be anxious," he concluded, "has learned the most important thing."

More recently, psychologist Rollo May likened anxiety to "the zest of the racehorse at the starting gate."[3] He observed that people who exhibited the highest levels of originality and creativity often felt the most anxiety.

Some of that is, no doubt, the anxiety provoked by responses to original, creative action itself. To be "creative" often involves defying conventional wisdom and acting contrary to

---

1. C. W. Saleeby, *Worry, the Disease of the Age* (Frederick A. Stokes Co., 1907).

2. Søren Kierkegaard, *The Concept of Anxiety: Kierkegaard's Writings, Vol. 8*, cited in *Historical Dictionary of Kierkegaard's Philosophy* (Scarecrow Press, 2001).

3. Rollo May, *The Meaning of Anxiety* (Ronald Press, 1977).

the norm. If others like the results of those actions, they label them "creative," but if they don't, they deem them—and the one responsible for them—"deviant."

In his controversial bestseller, *Listening to Prozac,* Peter Kramer took the notion of good worry even further. "What links men and women to God," Kramer wrote, "is precisely their guilt, anxiety, and loneliness."[4]

"And what would we be, we sinful creatures, without fear?" asked Jorge, the old blind monk in Umberto Eco's brilliant novel, *The Name of the Rose.* He called fear "perhaps the most foresighted, the most loving of the divine gifts."[5]

"Unselfish worry has been one of the saving forces of history," Saleeby asserted, "one of the greatest friends of mankind."[6] This quote takes on special resonance and meaning when we consider Christ on the cross, "worrying," suffering, and dying for us. It was love—not nails—that held him to that cross.

Our fear—especially our fear of death—gives life its meaning and focus, wrote psychologist/angler Paul Quinnett in his remarkable book titled *Pavlov's Trout.* After asserting that we all fear death, he continued, "To fish fully, we must fish in the face of death. This is good, not bad. To relish life means to know and to feel that it is always ending, not just for others, but for ourselves, too."[7]

Your goal, then, as you explore your worries and draw on God's teachings about worry, will not be to eliminate it completely. You couldn't even if you tried, and it wouldn't be good if you did. The well-lived life embraces concern for your-

---

4. Peter D. Kramer, *Listening to Prozac: A Psychiatrist Explores Antidepressant Drugs and the Remaking of the Self* (Viking, 1993).

5. Umberto Eco, *The Name of the Rose* (Warner Books, 1984).

6. Saleeby, *Worry, the Disease of the Age.*

7. Paul Quinnett, "The Existential Angler," in *Pavlov's Trout* (Keokee Co. Publishing, 1994).

self and for others, inviting a healthy level of "good stress." You will work, instead, to eliminate the negative, destructive, "bad worry."

But how will you know the difference?

Suppose two athletes experience anxiety before a crucial match. The first lets fear dominate him. His muscles turn to jelly, and his anxiety destroys his performance. Cruel fans call him a "choke artist" for failing to perform well under pressure. But the second athlete uses fear to focus his concentration and funnel his energy. He performs at or above his usual high level; the greater the stakes, the better he plays. We call such a star a "clutch" or "money" player.

One such star was Jerry West. Throughout a marvelous college basketball career at West Virginia and as an all-star guard for the Los Angeles Lakers, he earned the nickname "Mister Clutch." His teammates wanted him to take the last shot with the game on the line, and that was fine with him. He wanted the ball in his hands at those crucial moments. He made the "normal" shots, the ones he usually made, even under intense pressure. And occasionally he made the "abnormal" ones, once sending a playoff game against the arch-rival Boston Celtics into overtime by hitting a last-second shot from well beyond half court.

Michael Jordan was another, more recent, clutch performer. Many consider him to be the greatest ever to play basketball. Time and again Jordan hit the game-winning shot under maximum pressure. He once dominated a playoff game while suffering from severe intestinal flu. He didn't look for an excuse to fail; he invented a way to succeed.

Fear can sharpen our senses or freeze them. It can raise our awareness of and vigilance toward threats or it can lead to inappropriate behavior, apathy, even paralysis of the will.

Worry, if focused and purposeful, can drive you from your warm bed and propel you into productive activity—to create a masterpiece, to pray with passion, maybe just to change the kitty litter you had forgotten to attend to. (Not all our actions are performed on the stage of great drama. Some are simply necessary.)

But that same predawn concern may cause you to panic, the God-light of your creative energy focused not on a goal or vision but on vivid images of disaster. If you act at all at such times, your actions may degenerate into compulsive behavior, temporarily quelling the anxiety but never touching its true cause—so that you find yourself performing the same useless actions again and again.

In both cases you're awake when you "should" be sleeping. But you benefit from the first disruption and are hurt by the second. It's that second kind of anxiety, the crippling kind, which you're seeking to eliminate.

"Good" (that is to say "productive") anxiety produces an appropriate and proportionate response. For example:

- A car cuts you off in traffic. Before you can consciously react, you wrench the steering wheel, sending your car onto the shoulder of the road and you to safety. You feel deeply shaken, adrenaline punishing your nerves, and your terror produces a vicious headache hangover—but you've lived to tell about it.

- A stray dog snarls at you, baring its teeth. Before you've had time to decide what you should do, you back away. The dog, no longer threatened, leaves you alone.

- You're preparing to lead the weekly Scripture study, and the thought of standing up in front of the group terrifies you. But you fight your way through the fear, prepare carefully, and after the first few sentences, the icy anxiety dissolves.

Such responses are not only normal; they're necessary. You wouldn't survive without them. But "bad" anxiety may produce a response totally out of proportion to the stimulus and even render you incapable of acting. For example:

- The driver of the car behind you honks because you fail to respond instantly when the light changes from red to green. Enraged, you suppress the urge to leap from your car and confront the miscreant. But you seethe about the "incident" for hours, maybe even days.

- The neighbor's miniature Schnauzer yips at you from the window as you walk by on the sidewalk. You feel a surge of terror and decide to carry a gun with you the next time you walk around the block.

- You turn down an invitation to join the Scripture study, even though you'd really like to attend, because the idea of having to share your thoughts with others creates such intense panic in you.

We might label such responses excessive or inappropriate. (We would probably all agree that plugging that poor little Schnauzer—which, after all, is only doing his job—would be wrong.) But we'd better be careful about judging the appropriateness of anybody else's reactions. When Jesus advised us to "judge not, lest you be judged," he was making practical as well as moral sense. We can never know enough to judge another person's intentions accurately.

There is no "normal" or "baseline" tolerance level for anxiety, no "standard" reaction to danger or stress. You have your own internal gauges, just as I have mine. If your behavior seems to be a problem, and especially if it elicits responses you don't intend or want, then it is a problem, *your* problem. You need to seek solutions in prayer and Scripture, in self-help guides like this one, and perhaps even in counseling or therapy.

We will know the tree by the fruit it bears, Jesus tells us. Good worry should result in productive activity while allowing for a balanced life of rest, work, and play, a working partnership between faith and acts. Bad worry cripples the will and results in ineffectual activity or no activity at all.

But productivity alone isn't always a reliable guideline. Bad worry can drive you to frantic levels of activity. These efforts may earn you great rewards—a good job, a large salary, the respect of your peers—while tearing you down inside and building a wall between you and God.

If your anxiety pushes you into workaholism, your boss may reward you and your colleagues may rely on your sacrifices. Your family may appreciate and depend on the financial security and comfortable lifestyle your work produces. But you may shrivel and die inside, maintaining an energetic, competent façade right up to the breakdown.

Anxiety comes from stress, an internal reaction to life's pressures and challenges. External stressors—a demanding job, an unreasonable boss, a sick or dying loved one, a troubled child, the need to work two jobs to put food on the family table—produce internal stress.

Your level of stress depends on how many stressors you've been dealing with, how long you have had to deal with them, and how you have dealt with them. If the stressors don't ease, and if you don't deal with them effectively, anxiety may build to harmful levels.

Remember, any change, even good change, produces stress. Getting married, receiving a promotion at work, even winning the lottery can be as stressful as going through a divorce, getting fired, or sinking into debt. Holidays and vacations are stressful, because they overtax your energies and stretch your abilities.

You obviously need to temper the number of stressors in your life at any given time. Often, however, you really can't do much about those stressors. Sometimes life just piles them on! But you can do a great deal about the amount of stress they create in you and how you deal with that stress.

We'll get started on that worthy work in the next chapter.

"Do not anticipate trouble or worry about what may never happen. Keep in the sunlight."

— BENJAMIN FRANKLIN

CHAPTER 5

Faith Healing and Positive Thinking

"Lose weight with ease. No diets, drugs, surgery, or exercise."

Too good to be true?

Of course it is.

But we keep right on buying elastic belts and plastic suits and "all-natural metabolism enhancers" (uppers) to "magically melt the pounds and inches away—while you sleep!"

We keep right on wanting to believe, but heft springs eternal.

We teach our kids to "wish upon a star" and tell them that "wishing will make it so," but at some point, we stop believing it—at least with the rational part of our minds. Unfortunately, many come to feel the same way about prayer. "I asked God to help me lose weight" (or quit drinking or find love or get a better job or heal my husband of his cancer...), "but nothing happened. Prayer doesn't work."

Yet Jesus tells us that if we but have faith the size of a mustard seed, we can move mountains.

33

Does positive thinking work?

From Ben Franklin on, Americans have embraced the notion that a positive mental attitude can evoke a favorable reality.

In 1916, Charles Haanel published his *Master Key System,* describing the subconscious mind as a "benevolent stranger, working on your behalf."

"Would you bring into your life more power, get the power consciousness?" he wrote. "Live the spirit of these things until they become yours by right....You need not acquire this power. You already have it." [1]

In his 1936 book *Think and Grow Rich,* Napoleon Hill applied positive thinking to making money. "Riches begin with a state of mind," he wrote. You must "desire money so keenly that your desire is an obsession." [2]

Dale Carnegie's *How to Win Friends and Influence People* and Dr. Norman Vincent Peale's *The Power of Positive Thinking* were perennial bestsellers, and self-help books today continue to reiterate their themes.

Peale advised us to eliminate all negative ideas, rid ourselves of "worry words," and empty the mind twice a day, because "fear thoughts, unless drained off, can clog the mind and impede the flow of mental and spiritual power." [3]

According to Peale, Hill, and many others, we create a positive state of mind through autosuggestion. Chant your affirmation often enough, and you will come to believe it. Once you believe it, you will live it.

---

1. Charles Haanel, *The Master Key System in Twenty-Four Parts* (self-published, St. Louis, MO, 1916).

2. Napoleon Hill, *Think and Grow Rich* (Ballantine Books, 1987).

3. Norman Vincent Peale, *The Power of Positive Thinking* (Ballantine Books, 1996).

In 1978, Dr. Joyce Brothers—known to millions as a TV talk show regular—repeated this mantra in *How to Get Whatever You Want Out of Life,* teaching us to become "power people." That same year, M. Scott Peck hit the top of the bestseller charts with *The Road Less Traveled*—and stayed there for years.

On a more scholarly level, psychologist Abraham Maslow introduced "self-actualization," the process of achieving full human potential by transcending the ego.

Bobby McFerrin put it more succinctly in his 1988 hit song: "Don't worry. Be happy."

Werner Erhard (born Jack Rosenberg and a salesman by trade) developed a positive thinking boot camp called EST, where he drilled into adherents the notion that they have complete control over their lives and no responsibility for anybody else's.

An overweight, broke drifter named Anthony Robbins turned his life around and then told us how to do it, too, in books called *Unlimited Power* and *Awaken the Giant Within.* He became a national guru through videos, cassettes, and television infomercials.

Using positive thinking principles, Maxie Maultsby, Jr. wrote *Help Yourself to Happiness* and founded the International Association for Clear Thinking (ACT).

Other books promised to teach us to "have an out-of-body experience in thirty days." Seminar leaders coaxed us to walk on burning coals or broken glass. Computer programs in psycho-cyberspace promised to eliminate the need for time-consuming mantras or lotus positions with instant mind-alteration.

Wendy Kaminer called it all a bunch of nonsense.

"Americans do penance by buying books that criticize the way they live," she wrote in her 1993 *I'm Dysfunctional, You're Dysfunctional,* a scathing critique of the self-help movement.

Obviously criticizing the way we live, she characterized self-help monologues as the "babble of bliss speak, the elevation of feeling at the expense of rationality, the substitution of 'sanctimony for sense.'"[4]

The self-help hucksters preach simple solutions for complex human problems, she wrote. With no licensing or regulation in the "self-help industry," she concluded, millions were being defrauded by charlatans.

She told us, in essence, to grow up and stop believing in a psychic Santa Claus.

Kaminer found no dearth of targets. Wolves lurk in the self-help woods, just as surely as there are charlatan evangelists, crooked lawyers, and politicians on the take from powerful interest groups. And teaching folks to walk on hot coals or go out into the woods and beat on drums seems to beg for the ridicule of parody.

In her 1994 bestselling memoir, *Prozac Nation,* Elizabeth Wurtzel indicted not just the mentalists but also pharmacologists as well, warning of the nation's growing dependency on Prozac and other "feel-good drugs" to produce a synthetic sense of well-being.

But we need to be careful before we dismiss the whole notion of the power of positive thinking. The philosophy has no doubt helped millions of people gain greater confidence and control of their actions. I know a young man who was mired in depression, struggling with self-doubt, on the verge of throwing his life away. He had loving parents and a faith in God that somehow endured even the darkest times, and these surely sustained him. And yet, drugs and depression had him teetering on the edge of suicide.

---

4. Wendy Kaminer, *I'm Dysfunctional, You're Dysfunctional* (Vintage, 1993).

A street evangelist reading from the Bible late one night reached out to him. Alcoholics Anonymous brought him back from the brink. Tony Robbins helped him affirm himself and reorganize his life so he could cope even on the days when he felt like pulling the covers up over his head.

Self-help gurus like Robbins have their limits, but they can help people redeem their lives—no small thing.

Will praying make us healthy and wealthy?

In his book *Faith Is the Answer,* Dr. Norman Vincent Peale tied positive thinking to active faith in God, writing that the "ultimate method for having faith is simply to have faith." [5]

While Peale didn't directly promise that such active faith would make us rich and well, others have not been so shy. Dr. Frederick Eikerenkoetter started out as a teenage preacher in South Carolina, but soon transformed himself into "the Reverend Ike." He now bills himself as "senior pastor and presiding prelate...motivator, evangelist, and counselor to millions of people for over fifty years." He seeks to create in his adherents a more flamboyant "state of mind," bringing the fervor of the revivalist to the acquisition of wealth.

Using his "Thinkonomics," he promises to teach us the capital-T truth about ourselves and tap into the "Presence and Power of God within" to "learn how to become a more dynamic person...UNLEARN sickness and know health, UNLEARN money troubles and worry, and know success and prosperity."

But you have to work at it—by purchasing Ike's books, tapes, and videos, and by studying them diligently. Writing about his book, *A Science of Living Study Guide: Secrets for Health,*

---

5. Norman Vincent Peale, *Faith Is the Answer* (Fawcett, 1983).

Joy, and Prosperity, Rev. Ike notes on his website, "You must study it and practice the lessons on a regular basis. The Study Guide is not designed to be read only once and then put away. Spiritual growth and development involve continual study and practice. You will want to read it over and over."[6]

Not offering a quick, easy fix is commendable, but Ike is also offering himself an escape clause from his guarantees. The implied subtext is that if you don't grow healthy and prosperous, it's your fault because you didn't study enough.

Prayer and the power of suggestion

After editor and writer Norman Cousins suffered a massive heart attack, he rehabilitated himself through diet, exercise, and laughter. Watching tapes of old Laurel and Hardy movies helped him recover, he wrote in his book, *The Healing Heart.* If someone of Cousins' stature says so, perhaps we should listen.

When researchers test medications, they usually perform what's called a "double blind" test. They give the medication to half the subjects and a placebo (a sugar pill or some equally harmless substance) to the other. The subjects don't know what they're getting, and neither do the people dispensing the drugs.

In test after test, some of the folks taking the harmless (but also worthless) placebo show improvement. Did they improve because they believed they were getting real medicine, and the mere belief made it so? If so, does this mean we can talk ourselves into a healing frame of mind, as Peale, Carnegie, and Cousins suggest?

In Meredith Willson's delightful play, *The Music Man,* "Professor" Harold Hill convinces the people of River City,

---

6. Cf. www.revike.org.

Iowa, that he's teaching their children to play instruments by "the think system." If you want to play the "Minuet in G," you must simply think the "Minuet in G," Hill insists.

At play's end, Hill, the kids, and true love all triumph as the mighty River City Boys Band marches down the street, playing a thundering rendition of "Seventy-Six Trombones."

Pure hokum? Maybe not.

A tennis coach in Arizona taped his players' matches and created individual highlight tapes. Each athlete watched himself serve superbly, hit sizzling backhands, and return lobs. After watching the tapes, their play improved significantly.

In a controlled study, researchers had their subjects shoot free throws to establish a baseline level of performance (how many free throws each could make in twenty tries). A third of the subjects then practiced shooting free throws daily. Another third spent their practice time simply visualizing themselves shooting free throws perfectly—without ever actually touching a ball. The third group didn't do anything about free throws, physically or mentally.

When the subjects were tested again on their free throw proficiency, the group that diligently shot free throws every day did indeed perform better than before, as we would hope. Practice really does pay off. Also as we would have predicted, the group that didn't touch a basketball—or even think about one—showed no improvement.

But here's the shocker. The group that simply thought about free throws, without ever actually shooting any, also showed improvement equal to and in some cases superior to that shown by the group that had practiced.

Numerous other studies have reinforced the conclusion that positive visualization can improve athletic performance, public speaking, and a variety of other challenges. We know that it works, at least for some; we're just not sure how.

In the early 1980s, Dr. Larry Dossey, then a medical internist, learned of a study that seemed to show that patients in a coronary care unit who were being prayed for daily did better on average than patients not receiving prayers. Neither the nearly 400 patients in the study nor any of the doctors and nurses involved knew who had been assigned to the group receiving prayers and who was in the control group not receiving prayers.

Dr. Dossey searched through the literature and found more than 100 experiments on the impact of prayer. In more than half the studies he considered to be scientifically valid, prayer had a positive effect—on high blood pressure, cancer cells, tumors, even germinating seeds. He wrote about his findings in a book titled *Healing Words*.

Remember, now, the tests weren't about patients who prayed for their own recovery. The patients—without even knowing it—were being prayed for by others.

Many such tests have yielded no such positive and exciting results, however. The scientific jury is still out. The federal government has spent 2.2 million dollars in the past five years on studies related to such healings, with mixed, contested, and controversial results. As I write this, researchers are awaiting the results of a study led by Herbert Benson of Harvard University involving 1,800 heart-bypass patients.

Luke 5:17–26 describes Jesus teaching, "and the power of the Lord made him heal." In this passage, some men come to him, carrying a paralytic on a mat. The crowds are so great that these men can't get near the Master. So they go up on the roof and lower their friend on his mat through the roof. "When he saw *their* faith," Luke tells us (my emphasis), "he said, 'Friend, your sins are forgiven you.'"

So far as we know, the man on the mat didn't ask to be healed. The faith of his friends was enough to enable Jesus to heal him.

Remember the father who brings his son to Jesus to be healed of an unclean spirit (cf. Mt 17:14–19; Mk 9:14–29)?

"Lord, have mercy on my son," the man implores Jesus, "for he…suffers terribly; he often falls into the fire and often into the water."

The disciples tried to cast out the demon but were unable to. The man now turns to Jesus in desperation.

"You faithless and perverse generation," Jesus tells them, "how much longer must I be with you? How much longer must I put up with you?" And he asks the man to bring his son to him.

"If you are able to do anything," the man begs in Mark's Gospel, "have pity on us and help us."

"If you are able!" Jesus retorts. "All things can be done for the one who believes." Then Jesus rebukes the unclean spirit, and it immediately leaves the boy.

When the disciples ask why their efforts failed, Jesus tells them (in Matthew's account), "Because of your little faith. For truly I tell you, if you have faith the size of a mustard seed, you will say to this mountain, 'Move from here to there,' and it will move; and nothing will be impossible for you" (17:20–21).

Is Jesus really promising us, then, that we have only to call on him in faith, and we—along with our family and friends—will be healed of the evil spirits of mind and body?

We have all prayed, from the depths of our faith and need and love, for the sickness to pass, the storm to subside, the loved one to live. We have all suffered as our fervent petitions seem to go unheard. Does this mean our faith wasn't big enough—not even the size of a mustard seed? (Have you ever seen one? They're tiny!)

My wife and I were in a charismatic prayer group in Napa, California, when our friend Denise, a member of the group and also wife and mother of two, was diagnosed with terminal cancer. We prayed, individually and as a group, for her recovery. When she died, leaving a grieving widower and two motherless children, I heard someone say that God would have healed her if her faith had been stronger.

Jesus, however, tells us that we can't quantify faith and measure to see if we have "enough." He also tells us that we are not to test God.

The difference between thinking and believing

Where does positive thinking leave off and faith begin? Is positive thinking simply faith wearing a secular disguise? If so, faith in what? Will faith "work" in the same sense that positive thinking seems at times to work, calling forth a positive reality from a positive mindset? Will your faith ensure that all your earthly problems will be solved and that life will always go exactly as you want it to?

This is the critical juncture at which faith and positive thinking diverge. Jesus' trust in his Father led him not to riches and comfort on earth but to suffering and death on the cross. In the garden, despite his fervent prayer that the Father might "let this cup pass," he had to suffer humiliation, pain, and the death of a common criminal.

And his mother had to watch him do it. Her unwavering faith, her willingness to be the "handmaiden of the Lord," led her to the foot of her beloved Son's cross.

Faith leads us not to a pain-free life, but to the ability to stop trying to control all things and to trust God in everything.

Do we have "enough" faith?

"All things can be done," Jesus tells us, "for the one who believes."

"I believe!" the frantic father assures Jesus in Mark's account. "Help my unbelief!"

Clearly he has faith, or he wouldn't have come to Jesus with his petition in the first place. And we believe, or we wouldn't pray and participate in Mass and read Scripture. But the father in the story isn't sure that he believes enough, isn't sure his faith will be sufficient to merit a healing from Jesus.

And neither are we. From out of our faith ("I believe!") we pray for stronger faith ("Help my unbelief!").

In a sense, we are affirming Peale's simple tautology that the way to have faith is to have it. To refine the thought slightly, the way to have faith is to practice faith, to act always as if we believed in things not seen, even when we aren't sure our faith is sufficient.

For, in fact, you don't *have* faith in the sense that you "have" coffee beans in a canister in a cupboard, to be measured, ground, and brewed to produce the miracle of a good, hot cup of coffee. Faith isn't a commodity like coffee beans.

You *live* faith. Faith is your journey, not your destination. When you "walk by faith," you become the living embodiment of God's loving promise of salvation.

Your faith assures you that God is loving and kind and that his creation is good. Faith guides you toward the certainty that everything will work out according to God's plan, in God's time.

Faith isn't about getting rich or getting well or getting someone to love you. It isn't about "getting" at all.

Faith isn't about a quick, easy fix to life's problems. It isn't about "fixing" at all. Faith is your journey, your life, your essence.

God's promise is good the moment you claim it; in faith, the Father will always give you what you need. In faith, you will always find the Father's love for you even in the midst of tragedy, doubt, and denial.

In faith—and only in faith—you will find your peace and your ability to walk through the dark valley without fear.

> *"A day of worry is more exhausting than a day of work."*
>
> — JOHN LUBBOCK

CHAPTER 6

Why Time Management Couldn't Save Us from Ourselves

My friend Paul Ashe has run the Community Meal Program in Madison for twenty-five years. The project began when Paul and his friend Ralph Middlecamp began handing out free sandwiches at the Christian bookstore Ralph ran with his wife, Cathy.

Now the program serves lunch to 140 to 200 people four days a week and dinner to a like number five nights a week in a building called Luke House, which is owned by the program's Board of Directors. Different faith communities are each in charge of one meal a month. Volunteers prepare and bring the food, set up the dining area, serve the meals, and clean up afterward.

Some days we seem to be too few to get all the work done, but Paul cautions us not to hurry and not to try to do anyone else's job. He even directs us to work in shifts, so that everyone has a chance to sit down and have lunch along with the guests.

In fact, Paul says, sharing the meal is the most important part of the program—tearing down barriers between "them" and "us," recognizing our own poverty and our need to give, and having the grace to be served as well as to serve.

He tells the story of a student intern who spent a summer working with the program. "She never stopped moving, never stopped working," Paul says. She also never shared the meal with the others. One day, during the busiest part of the meal, Paul asked her to come to his office.

"I'm working," she protested.

Paul insisted. Once the woman was seated, he tried to explain his philosophy to her. She became agitated, picking up a Bible and waving it at him.

"It says here that we Christians are supposed to serve the poor," she told him. "And you're keeping me from doing it!"

He thought about that for a moment—Paul's a hard man to rattle—then asked her to come with him. He took her to where folks were standing in line, waiting for their turn to be seated and fed.

"What about them?" he asked, nodding toward the line. "Aren't any of them Christians?"

"Well, maybe *some* of them," she huffed.

"For some, sitting down and sharing a meal is the hardest part," Paul explains.

It's easier to work and keep busy, and the work separates "us" from "them"—the poor, the needy. As if we all didn't need each other!

Do you suffer from speed sickness?

We keep raising the speed limits, but we wind up stuck in traffic anyway, and it's driving us crazy.

Media began using the term "road rage" a decade ago to describe the kind of aggressive driving that includes unsafe passing, tailgating, yelling, rude gestures, and even gun play. In Seattle, a motorist blocked by traffic drove her car onto the sidewalk—and accidentally ran over a pedestrian.

The problem is serious enough to have prompted the National Highway Traffic Safety Administration to conclude that fully two-thirds of the nation's traffic fatalities—well over 40,000 per year—are directly caused by road rage.

We are a nation obsessed with speed, with getting there quicker, and with doing more in less time. We struggle to save time, buy time, gain time. We hate wasting time, killing time, and serving time. But more people driving more cars creates still more congestion, which means more waiting.

We hate to wait, but we're doing more and more of it.

We wait an average of an hour a day—for the elevator to come; for the computer program to download; for the voice message on the phone to finish so we can press one, two, or three; for the meeting to start; for the meeting to end.

A certain time manager estimated that over a lifetime, the average American will spend five years waiting in line, three years sitting in meetings, two years playing telephone-tag, eight months opening and throwing away junk mail, six more months sitting at red lights. And this was before the advent of e-mail! (How much time do you spend deleting spam?)

All our labor-saving devices were supposed to give us more time, but instead of being liberated, we spend *more* time— buying, maintaining, worrying about, learning how to use, and repairing all our gadgets. And we work longer and longer hours to make enough money to afford them all—while time to play, pray, and even sleep vanishes.

Our fax machines, e-mail, voice mail, instant messaging, text messaging, and the rest were supposed to help us communicate better and get our work done faster. But we're not working shorter days; instead, we've upped our expectations of how much we should get done in a day, working longer and longer while slipping further and further behind.

As the great baseball pitcher, philosopher, and social commentator Satchel Paige once noted, "The hurrieder I go, the behinder I get."

In the late 1800s, the sixty-hour workweek was the norm. By 1910, the average had dropped to fifty-one hours, and in 1929, as the stock market got ready to take its famous plunge, the average American was putting in forty-four hours per week between clock-in and clock-out.

By the early 1970s, the number bottomed out at about thirty-nine hours a week. With the onslaught of new technologies designed to make everything faster and easier, sociologists announced the arrival of the Age of Leisure.

But our perpetual vacation never came. Instead, we started working longer hours again. Now the average worker puts in about 164 more hours a year than he or she did in the 1970s. That's an extra month's worth of work. And after working those brutally long hours and enduring ever more hectic schedules all day, we bring more work home with us. No wonder so many of us work right through the Sabbath and have trouble sleeping Sunday night worrying about Monday.

Even when we seek a little fun, we don't relax.

Books are too slow and too much work—unless we can listen to them on CD while we're driving. We have easier and faster ways to get our information and have our stories told to us.

The VCR, TiVo, remote control, and other technologies let us fast-forward through slow spots, zap commercials, and graze from entertainment to entertainment. If a story doesn't grab us—right now!—we race to another. "I dare you to capture my attention," we seem to say, "but you'd better be quick about it!"

News has become just another entertainment—and just another symptom of the plague of speed sickness that's running unchecked through our culture. Television and radio reduce news stories to a minute or less, quotes to seven-second "sound bites." Print media break stories into briefs, sidebars, and digests. We don't read; we skim and scan.

The violent rhythms of football have replaced the gentle unfolding of baseball as our national sport, even as our lives become a series of two-minute drills to beat the clock.

We eat so fast, we barely notice *what* let alone *how much* we're eating. By the time our stomachs can get the signal back to our brains that we're full and can cease stuffing, we've consumed well beyond need or even satiation.

Nature itself has become too slow for us, so we capture and compress it with time-lapse photography. Perhaps we're so quickly destroying our precious earth in part because we no longer take the time to experience it.

Mismanaging time

Enter "time management" in the 1970s to save us from ourselves.

Books on time management have been around since at least 1910 and Arnold Bennett's *How to Live on 24 Hours a Day.* The modern time-management movement revived in earnest in 1973, just about the time the workweek was reversing direction and starting to lengthen again—and just as we were supposed to be entering that golden age of leisure. That's the year Alan Lakein gave the movement its classic text, the Q-source for all subsequent time-management regimens: *How to Get Control of Your Time and Your Life.*

You must "work smarter, not harder," Lakein told us. You need to exert control over your time by making a daily to-do list, assigning A, B, or C priority to each activity, and tackling the essential A items before going on to the Bs.

Use commute, coffee break, lunch, and waiting time productively, Lakein said. Handle paper once. Screen out the irrelevant. Say "no" to the time-wasters. Above all, keep asking yourself "Lakein's question": What's the best use of my time right now?

Lakein wasn't all about doing more, either. He warned against becoming a "time nut." He advised us to allow for flexibility by scheduling free time. Relaxing, he maintained, is a good use of time, and sometimes you can even get more done by doing nothing.

But we largely ignored this wisdom. Subsequent gurus of the clock-racer movement rushed to get their own versions of Lakein's formula into print without the warnings about overdoing.

A few good ones, like Tony and Robbie Fanning in their book, *Get It All Done and Still Be Human,* set as their goal feeling good rather than doing more. A few great ones, like Steven Covey in *The 7 Habits of Highly Effective People* and subsequent books, based life management on clarifying and adhering to your personal values system.

Most of the time management books, tapes, and seminars that followed Lakein stressed packing every minute of every day with as much "useful," time-efficient activity as possible.

Self-proclaimed experts advised us to become "polychronic" by learning to do two, three, four, or even five things at once. Workshops promised to help us manage "multiple projects, objectives, and deadlines." Time teachers told us to emulate champions of "polychronicity" like talk show host Joan Rivers, who had a speakerphone on her treadmill. Now, of course, such a concept seems almost quaint, as we walk around plugged into our cell phones.

We learned to work time to death. Instead of living, we schedule. Instead of listening to the inner voice, we hear the clock ticking. We aren't living in the moment. We're living in the next one, constantly trying to reach a horizon that keeps receding no matter how fast we run to catch it.

We wind up feeling wrung out, strung out, and stressed out.

At the end of another frantic day, when we should have time at last to lay our burdens down, we even shave time off sleep, so that eighty percent of us, according to most estimates, are now chronically sleep-deprived.

Getting back to fundamental principles

Did your mother ever give you a "time-out" when you misbehaved? Perhaps you had to sit quietly in a corner or go to your room while mom set the egg timer to measure your period of detention.

It was punishment then, but wouldn't it be a blessed relief now if someone could only give you regular time-outs or an occasional visit to Exile Island?

God does give us a time-out. It's called the Sabbath, and he commanded us to keep it holy. But we've turned the Sabbath into another set of projects and deadlines.

Remember when the disciples were accused of violating the Sabbath because they paused in a field to pluck off heads of grain to eat? "The Sabbath was made for man," Jesus told the Pharisees, "not man for the Sabbath" (cf. Mk 2:27).

God didn't create the Sabbath to punish us. He gave it to help us.

He didn't give us time to manage; he gave us life to live.

He didn't create us as slaves—to the clock or anything else; he created us as his sons and daughters.

God lets you decide how you will live your precious life. You get to choose not only what to do but also how much. You get to decide what's a "waste of time" and what isn't. If you make a schedule, you get to decide when to follow it and when to abandon it.

God gives us constant reminders to stay flexible and open to the moment, knowing that the most important things we do on any given day may not be on the to-do list at all. He gave me one such lesson, in fact, when I was in the midst of my initial study of time management. I had just learned the techniques for getting rid of "time-wasters"—in this case, people who waste your time with idle chitchat when you need to be working.

I was very busy. I was *always* very busy, much too busy for interruptions. So, when a former colleague appeared at my office door, I figured God was providing me with a marvelous opportunity to practice the techniques I was learning.

The man loved to talk—and he did it very slowly. Newly retired, he had lots of time for visiting.

Not with *me*, he didn't! I'd ease him right out the door before he knew what hit him.

I stood up rule number one—so he wouldn't infer a tacit invitation to sit. No way would I let him sit down; bodies in motion tend to stay in motion, but fannies in chairs tend to stay there. I moved toward the door—rule number two—to cut him off so he couldn't invade my territory.

Now I was in prime position to sweep my friend right out the door.

"Don't do it."

I'm not sure whether I really heard a voice in my head or only sensed the words; either way, the message was unmistakable: I was supposed to let him stay.

I didn't often heed such intuitions in those days, but for some reason I heeded this one. I backed off and offered the man a chair (while the voice I was more accustomed to hearing in my head shrieked, "No! Don't do it!").

He gently closed the door behind him and uncharacteristically came straight to the point. He'd been diagnosed with cancer and would be going in for surgery the following Monday. He hadn't told any of his other former colleagues, but he wanted to tell me because he considered me a friend.

He told me he was scared.

I didn't know what to say. I took his hands, he cried, and I told him I would pray for him. I think I might have cried a little, too. He talked for a few minutes more, then stood, heaved a sigh, thanked me, and left. He seemed to feel a little better, perhaps for having been able to share his burden, if only for a moment.

After he left I started to shake, realizing how close I'd come to dismissing him before he could share his terrible secret. When the phone rang, I was still so shaken, I just let it ring—an act of heresy for me in those days. (For the longest time, I didn't know that it's okay to postpone a telephone conversation until you're ready for it. That's why we have answering machines.)

That short encounter with a former colleague was one of those rare moments in life when we can truly be Christ for one another, and it certainly hadn't been on my to-do list.

I began to realize that I had a lot more choice about how to spend my time each day than I'd been exercising. You do, too.

Moment to moment, you get to decide—whether or not to answer the telephone, to take an unscheduled moment to talk, to respond to an e-mail, to watch television, to take a walk.

Like the Sabbath, e-mail and telephones and faxes are made for man, not man for technology.

From Stephen Covey, I'm learning to identify and separate activities that are truly important from those that are merely urgent. Nourishing my relationships with family and friends is important—though it rarely carries the feeling of urgency that propels me to drop everything to do something right now! Spending time in prayer and with Scripture is important. Calling 911 and then staying with an accident victim is important *and* urgent.

The ringing telephone, the beeping e-mail, the harried summons to "meet right away!" may or may not be important—but they always seem urgent. If we live only in the apparent crisis of the moment, we may never have time for the truly important things, the ones that nourish our spirits.

I'm learning to give myself enough time to do the job right, without panic. I'm learning to leave enough time for my trip across town so that I don't have to make a mad dash to hit every green traffic light and find a parking space immediately in order to get to my appointment on time. If I get stuck in traffic on the way—which is pretty much inevitable in my town—I welcome the wait as an opportunity to breathe deeply and pray.

I'm learning not to wait for vacations, weekends, or even the end of the workday to take a break. The build-up of stress is cumulative, and once you pass the "point of no return" on any given day, it becomes almost impossible to relax and get a restful sleep. You must break the tension cycle several times a day, with short breaks to pray, stretch your muscles, and ease your mind.

Don't let waiting frustrate you; turn a wait into a rest.

Can't find time to pray? That's because it isn't *lost*. You must make the time. If necessary, schedule a prayer break, even (make that *especially*) during the busiest of days. Read a passage from Scripture. Then meditate on what you've read, letting your breathing and your heart slow, so that you're able to sense the presence of God with you in the moment.

He's with us always; it's just that sometimes we're too busy to notice.

Forget about trying to become "polychronic"; don't try to become a master of multitasking. Relearn the wisdom and grace of doing one thing at a time, devoting all of your mind and heart to it. Perform even the most menial task in the service of the loving God who gave you life.

After all, what are we here for? What is that "one thing only" that Jesus told Martha to be mindful of? Isn't it to love and serve the Lord and each other, right here, right now?

When challenged to name the greatest commandment in the Torah, Jesus told us to "love the Lord your God with all your heart, and with all your soul, and with all your mind, and with all your strength" and to "love your neighbor as yourself. There is no commandment greater than these" (Mk 12:30–31).

Let these simple words become the basis for everything you do, every decision you make, and you can change the way you live each day. You can replace your old, time-centered responses with new, God-centered ones. The more often you succeed in this, the easier it will be to believe in the next success.

Anything of real worth or importance takes time. You might fall in love at first glance (I believe in it), but building a relationship takes a lifetime. The impulse to lose forty pounds, write a novel, or climb a mountain may come in an instant. But "crash diets" don't work, nor do "crash novels." There is no short way up the mountain.

Loving and serving the Lord is the work of a lifetime.

As the poet Donald Hall observed, we don't climb the mountain simply to reach the top; the joy is in the climbing.

What are you living for? Put your time and your heart where your values are.

CHAPTER 7

Casting Out Demons and Unclean Spirits

When Christ entered the land of the Gerasenes, the Gospels tell us, he encountered a man said to be possessed by an unclean spirit. Shackles couldn't hold this tormented soul, and he raged over the countryside, screaming and cutting himself with rocks.

As Mark tells the story (5:1–13), Jesus orders the demon out of the man and sends it into a nearby herd of swine at the demon's request. When Jesus asks the spirit its name, it responds, "My name is Legion."

Although no one else seemed to know who Jesus is, the evil spirits all seemed to recognize him on sight. Why was that? And why did Jesus warn them sternly not to reveal his identity?

The first miracle Mark reports after Jesus is baptized involves a man with an unclean spirit that shrieks, "I know who you are, the Holy One of God." Jesus rebukes him to "be silent, and come out of him!" (1:24–25)

What were those spirits? Were they misunderstood manifestations of mental and physical illnesses that we understand better today? If people were truly possessed by demons, do such demons still plague us?

Jesus passes on the power to exorcise demons to his disciples, establishing the biblical foundation for the rite of exorcism. But the disciples aren't always able to banish especially recalcitrant spirits.

"Why could we not cast it out?" they ask Jesus after one such failure.

"Because of your little faith," he tells them (Mt 17:19–20).

The Catholic Church still acknowledges demon possession and conducts exorcisms, as prescribed in the *Rituale Romanum,* although much more cautiously than in past times. The Pentecostals and other charismatic Protestant denominations also practice demon expulsion. Indeed, most major religions—including Judaism, Hinduism, Islam, and Shinto—have some form of exorcism ritual.

According to the Catholic Church, signs of demon possession may include fits and convulsions, "speaking in tongues" (*glossolalia*), displays of superhuman strength, and the ability to predict the future. As portrayed in popular movies, possession may also involve horrible stenches, a rasping, guttural voice, and even levitation. The one primary basis for declaring a person possessed is that person's sudden, violent revulsion toward sacred objects and texts.

Modern science can explain many of these symptoms. Seizures and convulsions may indicate epilepsy. Schizophrenia may account for other manifestations. People possessing knowledge of the future may have the gift of clairvoyance.

The demons of mental illness

Several members of my immediate family are or were alcoholics. Many have suffered from depression and manic depression (a term I prefer to the euphemistic "bipolar"). I was diagnosed with obsessive-compulsive disorder a dozen years ago and have undergone therapy and been on medication ever since.

Our most fervent prayers weren't able to banish these illnesses. We have required and still require medical intervention to provide if not a cure, at least a way of alleviating and coping with our illnesses.

We have sophisticated names for such things now; indeed, the number of named mental illnesses, conditions, and syndromes has grown at an astonishing rate in recent times. Along with schizophrenia, manic depression, and obsessive-compulsive disorder, we diagnose and treat generalized anxiety disorder, panic disorder, posttraumatic stress disorder, and hundreds of individual phobias, defined as extreme and persistent fear of specific objects or situations, including heights, enclosed spaces, open spaces, clowns, and the number 13.

Even so, many illnesses continue to defy diagnosis and treatment, folks continue to suffer, and troubling questions persist for believers.

- Why doesn't God simply heal us when we call on him?
- Where is God in our suffering?
- What if he is answering our prayers—and the answer is simply "no"?
- Does God afflict us with these mental plagues as punishment for our sins or the sins of our forebears?

Jesus and the disciples encountered a man who had been blind from his birth. "Rabbi, who sinned, this man or his parents, that he was born blind?" the disciples ask (as recounted in Jn 9:1–6). In other words, whose fault is it that he's blind?

Jesus answers the either/or question with a third option. "Neither this man nor his parents sinned," Jesus says. "He was born blind so that God's works might be revealed in him."

The man was afflicted, Jesus seems to be saying, so that God's saving grace might be revealed. Jesus then cures the man, touching off debate and consternation among the Pharisees.

Clearly, calamity, up to and including demon possession, happens to "good" people. Mary Magdalene was cured of multiple demon possession (one of the few things we really know about her) and became one of the Christ's most beloved and trusted disciples, the one to whom he first appears when he rises from the dead.

That other Mary, the virgin Mother of God, born without sin and entrusted with bearing and nurturing Jesus, proclaims herself to be the "handmaiden of the Lord." And her earthly "reward" seems to be the sight of her beloved Son, tortured and dying on the cross.

I have suffered little calamities of my own, of course, and I'm old enough now to have lost my beloved parents and many good and wonderful friends. Denise, Mark, Carol, and Steve in particular died much too soon by any worldly reckoning, and their deaths were painful and prolonged. Denise and Mark each left a spouse and young children behind. Steve was a priest whose good works extended far beyond his job as head of the Diocese of Madison Office of Education. Carol made beautiful music for liturgies.

In each case many believers prayed that they might be spared, and in each case God's answer seemed to be "no." At such times, those of us left behind might doubt, might rage, might ask in righteous indignation, "Why them?" (and, of course, in our suffering, "Why me?").

My pastor, Father Randy Timmerman, suggests that instead of asking "Why me?" we should be telling God, "Use me." My friends taught me much in their dying about faith and acceptance; perhaps it's my job as a surviving friend to manifest and use their teachings in my life.

Our worldly afflictions are in fact only unjust and outrageous if we view life as a physical phenomenon ending in death. But if life is fundamentally a spiritual journey, and if at death we are reborn into new life in the presence of God for eternity, then whether we live to be 24 or 40 or 102 becomes much less significant.

Do God's mysterious ways include Prozac?

You experience anxiety in your daily life. If you didn't, you wouldn't have sought out this little book. You may feel uneasy, tense, edgy, and nervous. You may find it impossible to relax and have trouble falling or staying asleep. Vague feelings of apprehension may make it hard for you to concentrate or even breathe easily. All these are typical symptoms of anxiety, most are brought on by specific stresses, and you can learn to deal with them effectively using the techniques we'll review at the end of this chapter.

But what if your "symptoms" seem to exceed this sort of treatable anxiety? What if they persist for an extended period of time and for no apparent reason?

Instead of relatively mild anxiety, you may experience intense and sudden fear, which strikes repeatedly and without warning. Your heart may start to pound, and you may experience chest pains, dizziness, nausea, and shortness of breath. You may even begin to shake uncontrollably.

You're experiencing a panic attack. If such attacks become severe enough and frequent enough, they can be disabling.

Like the gradual blindness brought on by glaucoma, symptoms of mental illness and disorder may manifest themselves gradually. Your shyness in social settings may become more acute over time. You may become increasingly anxious even with friends and in more familiar, safe, and anonymous social settings, such as shopping for groceries. At some point you may cross an invisible and poorly defined line between anxiety and illness. If left untreated, the mental illness of agoraphobia can leave you a prisoner in your own home, in a single room of that home, or even in one corner of that room.

Before that happens, and while you still can, you need to get help.

"Seek professional help" is easy to say. Advice columnists say it often. But it is in no way easy to do. It requires courage, determination, and persistence. Ironically, depression robs us of these assets, replacing them with a feeling of hopelessness that can merge into despair. You must act as if you believed help was possible, even if you don't in fact feel that belief.

First you must admit that you need help, that something in your life is beyond your control. If you tend to be a self-reliant problem solver, this can be extremely difficult.

Surmounting that hurdle, now you must confront and learn how to access the mental health system. Where do you start? Whom do you call? Do you need a medical doctor for a referral? Will you be seeing a counselor, a psychologist, or psychiatrist, a general mental health practitioner, or a specialist? Will treatment be covered under your health care plan? There's simply no easy way here. Start with your own medical doctor or a county mental health clinic for basic information and orientation.

If you have a loved one precede you into the mental health maze, as I did, you can rely on that person's counsel and support. No one on earth will understand better how hard this step is for you.

Otherwise, you might feel utterly alone at this point. Perhaps no one you know ever talks about mental illness. (It remains one of the great taboo subjects in our culture.) Watching other people functioning day to day all around you, and not knowing that some of them are undoubtedly dealing with mental health problems too, you may conclude that you're the only one on the planet who has the problem. (You'll be wrong, but that won't stop you from feeling it.)

Constant prayer is always important; at times like this, it becomes even more critical. Jesus is walking the journey with you, step by step. Call on him for his love and support. He will not fail you.

Help may come from unexpected sources. If you can summon the courage to talk about this new step in your development with a trusted friend or family member, you may get a surprise.

"Your Uncle Charlie has OCD, too. Didn't you know that?"

"My best friend was diagnosed with clinical depression three years ago. When he finally got help and went on meds, I couldn't believe the change in him!"

"You're manic? Hey, join the club. I've been in treatment since 1997."

Through my job with the university, I coach a lot of writers, and sometimes their writing delves into the deepest aspects of their lives. I've been honored to share their revelations of mental illness. They experience such relief and even joy when I reveal to them—as I now do, by the way, without hesitation or qualm—that I have a mental illness and that I've learned to function with it.

In fact, I believe that this is one of the primary ways I've been blessed to let God use me and my illness. The more I reach out and connect with other folks who are on a similar journey, the more joy and affirmation I receive.

Do I ever wish I didn't have obsessive-compulsive disorder? With all my heart. Even when controlled, it's distracting at best, exhausting and depressing at worst. Do I still have dark moments when I curse myself for being "not normal," for requiring medication just to be human? I do. Not nearly as many moments as I once had, however, and not nearly as bad when I do. Do Prozac jokes still annoy me? Yeah, they do. But sometimes now I'm able to turn them into an opportunity to do a little educating about a subject I happen to know all too well.

I needed a professional—a whole team of them, in fact—to pull me out of the hole. This isn't always the case with everyone. Alcoholics Anonymous still serves as the worldwide model for a successful self-help program, addicts helping addicts, without hierarchy or paid professionals, in mutual caring and respect. They support each other's quest for sobriety one day, one meeting, sometimes one moment at a time.

AA and other successful twelve-step programs begin with the basic admission that the supplicant needs help and that a Higher Power can give them that help.

Twelve steps for coping with "normal" anxiety: A quick review of anxiety-alleviating techniques

Okay, we needed to cover that information, and I'm glad we did. But the fact is, you may very well be able to deal with your fears and anxieties without intervention. Here's a little twelve-step program for taming the everyday demons, which are surely legion.

Most of this is classic time and stress management technique. I'm not a good manager, but I've learned to do what I need to do to get my work done and still have time and energy for family, friends, and recreation and to consciously spend time in prayer and with Scripture.

If I don't, two very bad things happen. First, I wind up taking time away from sleep and relationships by default. Second, I put off the difficult and the downright repulsive jobs (for me, that includes pretty much anything having to do with finances) until the pressure to do so becomes nearly unbearable.

I've found that it's worth imposing a little planning and discipline on myself. It turns out to be much less stressful in the long run.

Step 1:   *Understand that anxiety is a normal reaction to stressors and give yourself permission to feel it.*

Franklin Delano Roosevelt had it right: "We have nothing to fear but fear itself." Don't panic about panic. It's normal, healthy, even necessary.

Step 12: *Know that feeling the anxiety is all you have to do about it.*

You don't have to do anything to "fix" it. In most cases, it will simply go away by itself. Don't fear it. Don't fight it. Just feel it. Then go about your business.

Step 3:   *Downshift on the steep grades.*

"Slow down," my daddy always used to tell me. "You'll last longer."

When you feel yourself becoming super-stressed, will yourself to slow down. The more you feel like running, the more you should slow your pace and deepen your breathing.

There's actually a sound physiological reason why this works. When the brain detects some threat from the environment, it sets off alarms, pumping adrenaline and corticoids into your system, preparing you for fight or flight. Your heart rate and breathing speed up, and you achieve a state of heightened awareness. This automatic response, faster than conscious thought, allowed our forebears to survive in the wild, and it sometimes allows us to avoid that near-miss auto crash or some other assault.

When the brain sounds the "all-clear," the process reverses, and your system slows back down. Good thing. If you existed at a Code-Red level all the time, the stress would eventually corrode your immune system and open you up to illness and even premature death.

The process works in reverse, too. A hyper-physical state itself reinforces a sense of danger. "Fight or flight" can be a vicious circle. You get scared and start reacting, the reaction scares you, and you react even more.

By consciously slowing your breathing and calming your body, you send your brain the all-clear signal, and you begin truly and fully to relax.

It works in other areas, too. When something makes you happy, you smile. Conversely, if you smile, it can trigger the same chemical response in the brain, and the happiness follows. You're going to have to try this to believe it, but with a little practice, you'll convince yourself.

Step 4:   Take a vacation.

In fact, take four of them every working day.

Don't wait for the annual two weeks in summer. Don't wait for the weekend. Don't even wait for the end of the workday. Stress is cumulative. Once it builds past your personal point of no return, it's almost impossible to relax. It's a lot like a muscle cramp. Once it cramps, no amount of coercion will uncramp it. Only time will relieve it.

Take four stress-breaking vacations every day. Half an hour with a good book would be sublime. A ten-minute walk would be wonderful. But if these luxuries aren't possible, try two minutes of slow, gentle breathing with your eyes closed. Gently relax your shoulders and rotate your head to loosen your neck muscles. In 120 seconds, you can break the stress cycle and return to the wars relaxed and refreshed.

Step 5:   *Breathe from the belly.*

Speaking of breathing—don't forget to. I'm not joking. The more stressed you become, the shallower your breathing becomes. Soon you're panting like a dog with heatstroke. The brain doesn't get enough oxygen—but it does get the alarming message that you're under siege and may start firing off those adrenaline rockets again. In times of great stress, remind yourself to breathe deeply and slowly, from the belly.

Step 6:   *Pump some air into the schedule.*

You fill your schedules to the breaking point—and then extend the day to cram even more in. Soon you're racing from task to task. Constant hurrying trips the panic alarm, and any interruption can throw off the entire schedule.

How many days have you had lately without at least one interruption?

Don't schedule yourself so tightly that a disruption can flatten your house-of-cards.

Step 7:   *Schedule R & R.*

You're going to have to make time for those four mini-vacations, and at first you'll need to remind yourself to take them. Use sticky notes, computer prompts, an alarm clock, whatever it takes to get yourself to stop and breathe.

You may have to schedule "thinking time"; I build a telephone- and e-mail-free period into my workday, usually early in the morning.

You may even have to schedule time to talk to your spouse and kids or to spend with a friend. I know, it sounds strange. But if putting it on the calendar—and then honoring the appointment as much as you would a meeting with the boss or one of your clients—is the only way you can make the time, then do it!

Step 1:   *Talk out the problem.*

One of God's great gifts to us is someone with whom to share our burdens, someone with whom we can vent and moan and grouse—and be vented on in return.

Fact is, we all have one such friend in common. "What a friend we have in Jesus," the old song goes. If you haven't thought of him that way, picture the Good Shepherd, staff in hand, walking beside you, arm over your shoulder, listening intently to your worries and concerns.

I find the Good Shepherd to be such a comforting image, I usually don't even have to say anything to him. A little silent walk with the Man from Galilee often restores me.

You might also consider setting aside a few minutes at the end of each day or in the morning or at lunch to make a brief journal entry. Write whatever you're thinking about and feeling. There's no formula or format here.

Step 9:   *Give your movie a soundtrack.*

I used to go for days, even weeks, at a time without music in my life. What a mistake that is!

Now I often noodle on the piano for a few minutes before work in the morning. I put "the music of our lives" (music for—*ahem*—older people) on my office radio or play a favorite CD. When Father Randy took over as pastor of St. Paul's, he insisted that each daily Mass would include singing. "You're not going to walk out of here humming my sermon," he explained. Now I often walk back to the office humming or singing the healing Word.

Music is a fine tonic.

Step 10:   *Watch what you eat.*

No, this isn't a diet book, and I'm not going to start counting your calories for you. But I'm convinced that a healthy diet will help you mentally and spiritually as well as physically. Go easy on the fats and sugars and heavy on the fruits, veggies, and grains to keep the body happy.

Step 11:   *Keep moving.*

When I was eleven, I contracted rheumatoid arthritis and rheumatic fever. I was bedridden for months and hobbled for a long time thereafter.

My pediatrician, Dr. Deron Hosephian ("Doctor D" to my brother and me), dispensed encouragement along with medication, and he often repeated this simple piece of advice: "Once you're up and walking again"—and he never let me doubt that I would be—"keep moving."

He didn't tell me that my joints would stay more limber and my range of motion more fluid. (I was only eleven, after all.) He didn't tell me that exercise would keep my mind more nimble and my spirits higher as well. But I've found this to be the case all my life. Run, jog, walk, pace, pedal, but get yourself in motion whenever you can.

And when you do, again to quote the words of the sage Satchel Paige, "don't look back. Something might be gaining on you."

Step 12:   *Sleep.*

I'm a short sleeper. I get between six and seven hours of sleep on a typical night. I also take a nap in "big blue" (my beloved recliner chair) most afternoons when I get home from work. I get to sleep around 10:00 at night and usually arise between 4:00 and 5:00 in the morning.

Why in heaven's name do I do such an insane thing?

It works for me, always has. I'm lousy at sleeping in, was even in college (when I most certainly did not get to sleep around 10:00 many nights). This schedule suits me.

You need to do what works for you. You may require eight or more hours of sleep a night. You may be wide-awake and alert at 10:00 PM and something worse than dead at 4:00 AM. Chart your own rhythms and make your schedule accommodate them as much as possible.

Six days a week I pray, I exercise, and I write. On the seventh day I just pray and maybe do some of that reading I've wanted to get at all week. I've found a balance that works for me.

Your day won't look like mine, of course, and there's no reason to compare your schedule with mine or anybody else's. You simply need to find your own balance.

"Do not be afraid, little flock, for it is your
Father's good pleasure to give you the kingdom."

— LUKE 12:32

CHAPTER 8

Don't Sweat the Small Stuff

Writing a novel is like driving at night, author E. L. Doctorow once said. You can only see a little way ahead, but that's enough to get you where you're going. Having written several novels, I can attest to the fact that you can flash your high beams all you want, and follow the most detailed map you can find or concoct, but you're still going to find some surprises around every bend in the road.

Most of us like to know where we're going and what we're going to find when we get there. We study guidebooks and maps, plotting our course. We get our cars serviced before we leave and phone ahead for motel reservations to ensure a safe, comfortable resting-place each night.

No matter how much we prepare or how carefully we plan, we must at last submit ourselves to the unknown road, which will present us with experiences we didn't expect, good and bad, along the way. No matter how much we project ahead, we can only really experience the stretch of road we're on right now.

This is the wisdom the road imparts. Life is the journey, not the destination.

"One day at a time," Alcoholics Anonymous has been advising since Dr. Bob S. and Bill W. met in 1935 in Akron, Ohio. The original and much-copied twelve-step recovery program has helped countless people control their addictions and reclaim their lives, and its wisdom applies to us all. In AA, you don't try to stop drinking forever. You don't even try to stop drinking tomorrow. You "just" don't drink today. Tomorrow you get up and do it again. If you falter, you get up the next morning and commit that day to staying sober.

Each day is new, a fresh start. Each day God is there to greet you upon your rising. "The steadfast love of the LORD never ceases, his mercies never come to an end; they are new every morning; great is your faithfulness" (Lam 3:22–23).

Jesus taught us not to worry about tomorrow. He told us to ask the Father to "give us this day our daily bread," not to ask for a warehouse full of bread to last us a lifetime.

When Martha got so caught up in her serving chores that she had no time to spend with the Master, he gently chided her to take advantage of the precious moment, the sacred now. After all, the groomsmen don't fast while they still have the groom with them. The time to fast will come in God's time. One thing only is required: that we love God now, this moment. We must live and love in the present tense.

Separating the small stuff from the big stuff

Tony Robbins likes to cite this classic two-step formula for handling stress:

Step 1: Don't sweat the small stuff.

Step 2: Realize that it's all small stuff.

Los Angeles Dodger centerfielder Willie Davis handed the Baltimore Orioles the second game of the 1966 World Series when he made a record-setting three errors in a single inning. First Davis lost a fly ball in the sun and dropped it. Then he dropped another one, picked up the ball, and threw wildly past third base.

The defending world champs never recovered, losing to the Orioles in four straight games.

When the great Dodger announcer Vin Scully interviewed Davis after his disastrous game, he found a man at peace with himself.

"It ain't my life," Davis told him, "and it ain't my wife. So why worry?"

His life wasn't at stake. His relationship with his life's mate wasn't in jeopardy. He couldn't change the disaster that had occurred on the field. So even his performance in the most intense competition his profession provides was small stuff, not worthy of sweat.

It's also worth noting that the Dodger pitcher that day, Sandy Koufax, then the best pitcher in the game, came up to Davis after the inning of doom, put an arm of forgiveness around him, and told him not to let it get to him.

That's not to say that Willie Davis didn't care who won or lost. He just didn't worry after the fact. To a professional athlete like Davis, caring means conditioning mind and body to be prepared, honing skills through almost endless repetition, and remaining fully alert and in the moment on the field. Worrying means stewing about things you must do but are afraid you can't, or about things you did and can't undo.

Caring helps; caring is productive. Worry hurts and is counterproductive.

Contrast Davis's reaction with that of California Angel pitcher Donnie Ray Moore. In game five of the 1986 American

League Championship Series, Moore gave up one of the most significant home runs in baseball history. With the young Angels (now the "Los Angeles Angels of Anaheim") one strike away from earning a trip to the World Series, Oakland A's outfielder Dave Henderson spanked a game winning homer off Moore. The A's went on to win the next two games and the series.

Moore apparently brooded over his failure during the off-season, and, just in case he might try to forget it, the fans were brutal to him the next season. Two years later, Moore was out of baseball. He fell into alcohol abuse, his marriage faltered, and, in 1989, unable to bear his burden any longer, Donnie Ray Moore committed suicide. We can never know all the reasons behind the tragic act of a person taking his or her own life, of course, but Moore's inability to put this failure behind him may well have been a contributing factor in his death.

Okay, so you don't sweat the "small stuff," even small stuff like muffing two fly balls and overthrowing a base in a World Series game before millions of fans. But what about the BIG stuff, like the health and well-being of your family or your relationship with God? Do you dare to take a "don't sweat it" attitude toward the core values of your life? Shouldn't you sweat?

Only if sweating—worrying as opposed to caring—would help. But it doesn't. Not a bit. If you aren't convinced of that fundamental fact, or if you know it in your head but don't yet believe it in your soul, try the exercise in "Worryography" featured in *The Worry Workbook,* developed as a companion to this little text. Then start living as if you believed with all your heart that worry is destructive to your well-being. Bring your worry to God in prayer. Ask him to guide and strengthen you. He'll be there to help. Then, having turned it over to God, let it go.

All your worries, then, fall into one of two categories: small stuff, not really worth sweating, and big stuff, which even an ocean of sweat won't help. So turn all the stuff, big and small, over to God.

"Are not two sparrows sold for a penny? Yet not one of them will fall to the ground apart from your Father.... So do not be afraid; you are of more value than many sparrows" (Mt 10:29, 31).

Return to these nourishing words often. It's hard to worry while in the presence of such a loving, caring Father.

Saving yourself from doubt

You can no more banish worry from your life than you can save yourself from death. But God can do it if you let him. "For mortals it is impossible, but not for God; for God all things are possible" (Mk 10:27).

Bring that heart full of worry and anxiety to God. It's hard, isn't it? We're so accustomed to pretending, hiding our fears from a critical, competitive world. We're taught not to talk about it.

Our culture views worry as a sign of weakness, an indication that you're not in control of your life. You must say nothing if you're afraid that your spouse is falling out of love with you, or that your teenagers don't respect your values, or that you're developing a double chin, or that the next pink slip at the office will have your name on it. When someone asks how you're doing, say, "Fine."

So you remain silent—and go right on worrying, bearing the burden alone, and adding denial and guilt to the load.

Wait a minute! As Christians, aren't we already supposed to know that we're not in control of our lives? God's in control, remember? You didn't create the world; you didn't even "earn" entry into it. You can never know for sure what's around the next bend in the road, let alone your fate for eternity.

That's not to deny God's great gift of free will. You get to decide whether you'll eat a garden salad with low-fat dressing or a triple cheeseburger. You get to decide if, when, and whom you'll marry and where you'll live. You get to decide whether to try to conceive children or not. You even get to decide whether to accept or reject God's Word and will for you.

You can't walk the road toward perfection in God if you aren't free to choose that road or some other.

God also made you free to worry or not. You get to choose. He seems to have given some of us considerably more talent for worrying, to be sure. If you're one of these—and of course you are, or you wouldn't be reading this book—accept it. You're God's little fuss budget (and I am your soul brother). Respect, accept, and honor your feelings, including the "unacceptable" ones like envy, hatred, and, yes, anxiety.

We might not be able to help such feelings—at least not yet—although we can certainly turn them over to God for healing. God didn't command us to love our neighbors because we were naturally inclined to do so anyway. Being human, we feel all sorts of things about our neighbors that aren't anything like love. But we're commanded to express love, to act in love, to treat others as we want to be treated, regardless of our feelings.

Make the conscious decision to love—and to stop worrying.

Catching yourself in the act

To accept and deal with worry, you first have to catch yourself worrying. That may sound easy, but if you think about it, you know it's not. If you're like me, you've made a life's work out of trying to be perfect (which includes, of course, not being subject to anxiety). You've probably gotten very good at hiding your worries—even from yourself.

Oh, but the worry's there, all right. It may have gone underground, into your subconscious, surfacing in tension dreams and late-night "formless furies," and in physical symptoms from a stiff neck and a mild headache to high blood pressure and heart disease.

Instead of evading awareness of your anxiety, consciously face it and let it flood you. (Again, you may want to try the exercise of keeping a "worry journal" in the companion workbook.) Feel it all. Try to understand any deeper, fundamental fears that may be making you dread something seemingly innocuous.

Being that scared isn't easy! Hang onto the Lord in the storm! Pray these comforting words of the psalmist: "The LORD is with me; I am not afraid; what can mortals do against me?" (Ps 118:6).

Here's the double good news—and it's very, very good. First, you don't have to try to "solve the problem" of worry or even to understand it. It just is. Your job is to experience it, all of it. That's plenty enough work for the moment. Open yourself to your feelings, own them, embrace them, and accept them as part of who you are.

The second bit of good news is even better. The worry will go away by itself. In fact, the more you practice this exercise, the faster the anxiety will disperse into the vapors, leaving you with an almost giddy sense of lightness and freedom.

"We have faced the enemy," Walt Kelly (speaking through his creation, Pogo Possum) famously said, "and he is us."

You can conquer this enemy, unmasking it for the fraud it is, if you simply stop running, turn around, and face it.

Talk back to the worries that remain. Are things really that bad, or are you being unrealistic? We dismiss optimism as "wishful thinking" and elevate pessimism to the ranks of "realism." This is nonsense. Pessimism and optimism are subjective ways of viewing the world. They become habitual. Expectations of success are no less realistic than forebodings of doom.

Play the "what-are-the-odds?" game with your fears. Realistically, what is the likelihood of your worst fears being realized? What does your experience and the experiences of others teach you? Have you confronted a similar situation in the past? If so, how did it turn out?

If the worst really does happen, will you be able to deal with it? Underlying much of our worries is the implicit notion that we're incapable of handling the situations we worry about. But haven't you handled similar challenges in the past? You can handle the next one, too.

Let God guide you every step of this journey. Let his Word provide direction and blessed assurance.

The next time you feel your anxieties beginning to close in on you, shine the light of Scripture on them. Some of the psalms are especially good for this. Consider:

"I sought the LORD, and he answered me, and delivered me from all my fears" (Ps 34:4).

When the "formless furies" really have a hold on you, try:

"My heart is in anguish within me, the terrors of death have fallen upon me.... But I call upon God, and the LORD will save me" (Ps 55:4, 16).

He really will, you know.

"When I thought, 'My foot is slipping,' your steadfast love, O LORD, held me up. When the cares of my heart are many, your consolations cheer my soul" (Ps 94:18–19).

Repeat as often as necessary.

On the night before he died, Jesus prayed in the garden that he might not have to drink from the cup of death. God didn't remove the cup, but he did ease his Son's anxiety, enabling him to face his trial with the courage spawned of steadfast faith.

Our loving God will do no less for you.

"Any concern too small to be turned into a prayer is too small to be made into a burden."

— CORRIE TEN BOOM

CHAPTER 9

Meeting Worry Head-On

You've begun to develop the habit of identifying and talking back to your anxieties and submitting them to the power of prayer. Now you'll take another big step toward breaking worry's hold over you.

Get out your calendar and schedule worry time. Write the appointment down; you won't need more than about ten minutes.

I'm serious here. Go get the calendar. What's good for you? How's tomorrow morning at 7 AM?

You can begin or end your day with your worry time or use it as a tension reliever in the midst of a busy day. Consider scheduling your worry break at a time when you generally tend to be anxious anyway. (This probably corresponds with a dip in your energy levels.)

When I'm traveling, I often find myself flooded with anxiety right around sunset. So sundown on the highway is an excellent time for me to take a break from driving and give my full attention to my feelings. If first thing in the morning seems like a "good" (anxious) time, when the pressures of the day attempt to waylay you before you even get out of bed, you might try something like this:

7:10 AM Get up.

7:20   Feed cats, start coffee, retrieve newspaper, glance at front page.

7:30   Worry time.

7:40   Read newspaper, eat breakfast....

To help you get into the habit, it's useful to schedule the break for the same time each day, but this isn't necessary. If different days present different challenges and different time configurations, plan accordingly.

Whatever time you select, be faithful in keeping your appointment. If an emergency arises, of course you'll tend to that—but reschedule your worry break. If the "emergency" wouldn't have kept you from a meeting at work or a social engagement, it shouldn't keep you from your worry appointment either. Respect this worry time as fully as anything else on your calendar.

Suppose you schedule a worry break for Monday morning, right after the kids leave for school. (Maybe you're worried *about* the kids and school!) You're going to honor that time, but your worry won't. Worry won't wait. It will catch you while you're getting ready for bed on Sunday night and try to turn your restful, restorative sleep into a wrestling match with your demons.

When it does, you're simply going to send it away. Give it a rain check. Tell it, "Not now. I've got you scheduled for tomorrow morning at 7:40."

The worry will come storming back, of course. Don't panic—and don't think you've failed. This is the nature of worry. Tell it to go away. Tell it again. Keep telling it every time it returns, assuring it that you've scheduled time for it the next morning.

The worry will get subtler, seeping into your subconscious thought and even into dreams. When you catch yourself wrestling with that worry, don't chide yourself, and don't despair. Just send it away again.

It takes lots of repetition. You've been building your worry pattern for a long time, so long that worrying feels natural, an automatic part of your conscious thought. Be patient and forgiving with yourself. Pray often and turn to Scripture for comfort and guidance. Try Philippians 4:6–7, which tells us:

> Do not worry about anything, but in everything by prayer and supplication with thanksgiving let your requests be made known to God. And the peace of God, which surpasses all understanding, will guard your hearts and your minds in Christ Jesus.

In time (give yourself several weeks to develop the habit) you'll actually start training your worries to come on schedule. You'll be able to enjoy the rest of your life more fully, focusing your energies on work and worship, relationships and recreation, rather than on useless worry. You'll be more fully present to loved ones, friends, colleagues...and yourself. You'll experience the power of focused living in the moment.

Eventually the worry sessions themselves might become unnecessary, but that isn't the goal. You can go on scheduling your worries for as long as you need to.

While you consciously banish your anxieties between worry sessions, your subconscious mind will ponder possible solutions. We don't really understand how this incredible gift from God works. We're not even sure what to call it. Perhaps Charles Haanel came closest, way back in 1916, when he called the subconscious a "benevolent stranger, working on your behalf."

Understand it or not, the subconscious constantly plays with images and ideas, with total disregard for natural law, morality, and ethics. That's why "you" can have a dream "you" neither approve of nor even understand. The subconscious happily breaks all the rules that govern the waking mind. You can't control the process, but you can give it time to happen, and you can pay attention to its rich yield.

Facing down the monster

Worry time is here. The kids are off to school. You've unplugged the phone (or perhaps you've developed the will power to let the answering machine pick up when you're busy) and done your best to eliminate other potential distractions. Now what? Just how do you take a worry break? Should you have a special place for worrying? Will music help? If so, what's the best music to worry by? What's the proper worry position—sitting, standing, or lying on a couch? What's the best technique? How should you breathe while you worry?

The right way to do it is *your* way. Set a timer for ten minutes, so you won't have to look at a clock. Get comfortable, so your body won't interrupt you. Quiet your mind, freeing yourself from distractions. Prepare to let your worry come flooding in.

You might be scared. Any step into the unknown is frightening, especially confronting something you've tried so hard to avoid. Author Amy Tan writes of being so terrified, she felt as if her fear were literally chasing her. She had to learn to stop running and turn and face the monster, even while her every instinct screamed for her to keep running.

You've stopped running at last. Now just let the worry happen. Simply experience it, all of it. Don't fight it. All you have to do for the next ten minutes is pay full attention to it.

Doing this kind of nothing may be one of the toughest tasks you'll ever do, especially at first. Open yourself up to the full force of the anxiety. Feel it all. Allowing yourself to be flooded with worry can feel like being battered by an inner tsunami. When I first started doing this, I felt as if an electric current had passed through my shoulders and head; I even experienced violent muscle spasms.

You may feel yourself spiraling into a dark pit. Let yourself fall. Christ is with you. Nothing bad will happen to you. The feelings can't really hurt you; only the constant strain of fearing and fighting them can hurt.

Don't rush it. Let the fear run its course. The storm will subside, replaced by a sense of great relief much deeper than the mere absence of fear. You will have survived the worst the worry can do to you! You've embraced the monster and emerged not only unhurt but also more whole than you were before.

"Silly me, to have been scared of being scared," you might think. But you weren't being silly; you were being human. We're all afraid to be afraid.

Take a moment to thank God for being with you in your worry and for seeing you through safely. (Never doubt that he was there the whole time.) Thank God for the worry itself. The worry is a part of the gift of your life, part of the energy and life force that make you who you are. Embrace it all.

You're a worrier? Me, too! Now let's get on with our lives.

Ah, but don't get smug. You've only banished worry temporarily. It will return. It might have been humbled by its failure to shake you loose from your faith, but it might make an even stronger assault on your psyche. Tell it to go away until the next worry session. Do this long enough, and the worry won't bother you.

What if you sit down to your worry appointment and the worry doesn't show up? You say, "Come and get me," but no monster appears; no hurricane envelops you. Perhaps you're still fighting subconsciously, unable to relax your lifelong guard against letting yourself experience your anxiety. That's not really surprising, is it? After all those years of defending yourself, it's hard to lay down your arms and face the enemy without sword and shield.

Use your worry time to pray. Make another appointment. Go on to whatever's next in your day.

The worry will no doubt show up the moment you get up. It wasn't gone, only hiding. Send it away and wait for the next appointment.

When you and your worry next meet, our saving Lord will again be with you, guiding you through the darkness of worry into the light of true peace. He will never abandon you, never fail you. Trust in him.

Chapter 10

Moving from Worrying to Doing

When champion cyclist Lance Armstrong was struck with testicular cancer, he acted. He sought treatment, rehabilitated, and then began training for his next Tour de France—which he won!

He may have been worried or scared or even terrified—but he acted.

You probably don't need to turn to such a public example to find a person in your life who exhibits great courage in the face of a terrifying reality.

My father has always served as that example for me. The son of Belgian immigrants, he was born in this country but made the long voyage back to the homeland with his parents to get his older sister, Suzie. He returned to America—for all intents and purposes an immigrant himself—when he was still less than two years old. He grew up in a slum, spoke no English until he started school, and was beaten by gangs if he strayed into the wrong neighborhood.

When one of the worst labor struggles in American history closed the silk mills along the Passaic River, my grandfather lost his job and had to go to work in a slaughterhouse. He drank, abused, and eventually deserted his family. My father had to steal coal from the freight trains in the local yard to heat his family's home.

Such a wretched childhood might have knocked the dreams out of him and created one more street thug. Instead, he worked to support the family, delivering newspapers and taking on a milk route before school. He got top grades; played football, baseball, and basketball; and starred in track.

This earned him an appointment to the United States Naval Academy where, as he often liked to say, he became "an officer and a gentleman, as certified by Congress."

He served in the Navy for twenty years, retired to raise a family, and built a second career as part of the post-war construction boom in Los Angeles.

But of all his accomplishments, what most amazes me about this man, my hero, was how devoted he was as a father to my brother and me. He was always there for us—Scouts, sports, and studies—even passing up job promotions if they would take him away from his family. He taught us skills with gentle coaching and by letting us own our failures, and he taught us by example the virtues of hard work, determination, and absolute honesty and integrity. All this without having had a father role-model of his own to show him how, or even to let him know that such fathering was possible.

A remarkable man, my father took all his anxieties and converted them into steadfast, determined action.

I've been blessed with role models throughout my life. I now teach in the Odyssey Project here in Madison. It's an outgrowth of a program called the Clemente Course (named for the baseball player Roberto Clemente, himself a great role model) and was started by a man named Earl Shorris in New York City.

Each year, Director Emily Auerbach selects a class of thirty students (from among ninety to 100 applicants) for a special six-unit college humanities class. You must have a high school diploma or equivalent to qualify, and you must be living at or below the federally defined poverty line.

As you might expect, many of our students have survived great hardships; in some cases, their stories are all but unspeakable. They learn to speak and write these stories and to trust each other with them. One of the students in our first class three years ago wrote of her experiences as a drug addict and prostitute. Another needed bus fare so she could leave the Salvation Army homeless shelter in San Antonio and come north with her two children. A third saw his fourteen-year-old cousin gunned down in the projects of Chicago where he grew up.

What courage it must have taken just to go on living—let alone decide to go to college. What courage it takes to admit that you can't read your textbook, that you've never heard of Frederick Douglass or Henry David Thoreau or Socrates, and that you can't even write a coherent sentence.

Many of these profiles in courage become stories of redemption. Most do make it through a rigorous year of study, building skills and confidence and finding their voices. Many go on to seek more education. Several are on the honor roll at the local technical college, and two made Phi Theta Kappa, the honor society of two-year colleges. This spring, one of our first-year graduates earned her degree from Edgewood College here in Madison, our first four-year college graduate.

Many other people in my life demonstrate courage in action: Senator Russ Feingold, author/journalist John Nichols, attorney/activist Ed Garvey, Brother Joe Maloney, Sister Susan Slater, and my wife and my son, to name just a few.

can your role models teach you about acting in the ~~of~~ your fears? How can you emulate them?

Escaping the escapes

In the face of the overwhelming, often undefined anxieties of life, some seek escape in drugs (I put alcohol at the top of this list) to relieve tension. Others use television, sex, video games—anything to keep them from feeling and confronting their pain.

One of the most pervasive drugs in our culture is hyperactivity and its accomplice, multitasking. We carry our laptops and cell phones everywhere so we can be available 24/7. We rely on our crowded day-planners to get us through each day. We create endless to-do lists. Got a blank space on the calendar? Plug it. Keep moving. If you aren't exhausted at the end of the day, you must not be carrying your weight.

It's madness. It can also be very destructive—physically, mentally, and spiritually.

You'll never confront your fears unless you stop running. You'll never embrace true freedom in the love of God if you rely on all those painkillers to numb you and if you move so fast, you become unaware of the choices and possibilities God offers you each day. You must admit your addiction and shun the drug.

For more persistent and subtle anxieties, you may need to probe for the specific cause. I often discover the true source of my anxiety by presenting myself with mental images and letting my "emotional Geiger counter" tell me when I've found the real anxiety provoker masquerading as something else. For me, that Geiger counter is a fluttering in my chest or a burning in my stomach. It may manifest itself differently in you, but you've got one. You just have to learn to pay attention to it.

Once you recognize the source of your fear, turn it over to God in prayer. Pray as Jesus did in the garden: "Your will, not mine, be done."

With God's guidance, determine what you can do about the cause of this anxiety. Don't evade it. Act in the face of your fear, knowing that God is with you in your struggle. Only when you act in the face of your fear can you grow beyond it and into increased wisdom and self-assurance.

What about those times when there's really nothing you can do?

Do nothing. Experience and identify the anxiety—thus robbing it of much of its power—and move on.

"But I've always been a worrier," you say. "It's just the way I am." I understand. I've always been a worrier, too. But it isn't "natural" to obsess this way. I learned to be a worrier, and so did you. We learn to expect the worst and to believe that we are incompetent to deal with life. We can learn to replace worry with faith in action and to expect positive results.

Acknowledge your fear as a sign that you're fully alive and fully in the moment. Use its energy to empower you to act. You can transform worry into anticipation, fear into excitement, and both into action.

Next time anxiety erupts, review these six steps for turning anxiety into energy.

Step 1:   *Don't resist or deny the fear.*

If you do, you'll only send it underground, where it will fester and grow stronger, to resurface and attack you when you're most vulnerable. Face your fear. Let it wash through you. Feel all of it. As you stop fearing the fear, the panic will subside. Worry will have done its worst to you, and you will have survived intact.

Step 2:   *Give form to the fear.*

Sometimes fear comes disguised as the "formless furies"—vague dread that can shake you out of a sound sleep and leave you wide-awake until daybreak. Or it may take on a specific but false aspect. Track your fear to its true source. (One therapist calls this "tying a string to it" to see where it leads you—perhaps even all the way back into childhood.) Give it a name. You might even write down the worry, being as specific about it as you can.

Sometimes merely bringing the fear out of darkness and into the light can cause it to vanish. If not, having named it, you can begin to deal with your fear effectively.

Step 3:   *Push the fear to the extreme.*

Your fear doesn't exist apart from you. It's a reaction that takes place inside you. You created it, and you can use, rechannel, or even diffuse it.

Ask yourself two questions:

What's the worst that can happen?

What are the odds that it will?

You may be able to see that your level of fear is unjustified, that you can survive the worst, and that it isn't likely to happen anyway. But if this exercise doesn't dissipate the fear, move on to the next step.

Step 4:   *Figure out what, if anything, you can do about it.*

Brainstorm all your options (including the option to do nothing). Play with the possibilities. Write down everything that occurs to you, even the impractical and just plain silly. Submit your decision to prayer. Let God help you choose the option that seems best.

Write down exactly what you've decided to do and when you intend to do it. Don't be vague here. "Sometime after the kids go off to college" won't cut it. We're talking "Thursday afternoon at 4:00."

Now get about your business.

When the worry comes back, which it surely will do, gently remind yourself, *"I've already decided what to do about that."*

You may be wasting your time and psychic energy worrying about a decision you can't really make yet. If that's the case, tell yourself, *"I don't have to decide that now."* Repeat as often as you need to. Write down when and where you will decide. Give the problem back to your subconscious and let your subconscious play with it.

Now here is a critical piece of this step, one that will seem extremely counterintuitive (a fancy phrase for "flat-out wrong"!) the first several times you do it. Tell yourself, *"Whatever I decide will be fine."* Say it until

Six steps for turning anxiety into energy

1) Don't resist or deny the fear.

2) Give form to the fear.

3) Push the fear to the extreme.

4) Figure out what, if anything, you can do about it.

5) Act in spite of your fear.

6) Abide by your decision and its consequences.

you believe it. You're not brainwashing yourself, because the statement is true. Submitting your problem to prayer, making a decision, and moving forward is the right thing to do. The only wrong move here is no move; don't let yourself stay paralyzed by fear.

If you can't believe that anything you might decide could possibly be "fine," act as if you believe it and move forward to the next step.

Step 5:   *Act in spite of your fear.*

Here's one of those little secrets about life that changes you forever once you catch on to it. We all figure we're the only ones who are worried. You think it. I think it. The President of the United States probably thinks it (whoever's in office when you read this). You feel your fears, but you see only the composed masks, the "game faces" of others. So you figure they've got everything together and you're the only one floundering. It isn't true. We're all struggling.

Remember, others can't see your fears, either. By this stage in life, you've gotten very good at appearing composed in public. It's an adult bluff, one we start mastering as soon as we go to school, and we're all running it.

Folks figure you're cool, calm, and collected unless you choose to tell them otherwise.

Courage, then, isn't lack of fear. Courage is acting despite your fear, rechanneling that fear into positive energy and a mental state of hyper-alertness. Don't pretend you're not afraid. Experience your fears fully, knowing that they're universal and that God is present in them. As the fear runs its course, a gentle sense of peace will replace it.

Often you must act before you feel anything resembling peace. Take several deep, cleansing breaths. Expect a positive outcome. Then act as if you're no longer afraid.

Step 6:   *Abide by your decision and its consequences.*

Make each decision only once. Whatever you do, do it wholeheartedly, put your all into it, and then get on with your life. If you're not getting the results you want, then make a new decision and act on it. But set this decision aside once you've made and acted on it. You're finished with it. A lot of folks make an excellent living in our society second-guessing others, but you won't benefit one bit from second-guessing yourself.

No more running away. Breathe deeply. Pray. Listen. When you break the momentum, anxiety can't chase you. It can no longer rob you of the quiet goodness of living and of a rich appreciation of God's creation and your place in it.

If you fill each moment with fear and with evading that fear, you leave no room for the Spirit to work in you, no chance to hear God's voice and discern his will for you. God speaks in the still, small voice, but the tornado of activity can drown it out.

You won't eliminate all worry. You wouldn't want to. You will seek out and confront your anxieties. When you do, you'll be able to use them as energy, responding to life's challenges. You'll be free to live a Spirit-directed life.

If you worry about tomorrow—a phantom that exists only in your mind—you fail to live today, which is rich and real and contains all you have and all you'll ever need.

You don't need tomorrow to make you whole or to give your life meaning. You are whole in this moment. You have everything you need—right here, right now. God will teach you everything you need to know.

This isn't wishful thinking or blind optimism. It's the fundamental truth of your existence in Christ. You have only to claim it

*"I have learned to live each day as it comes
and not to borrow trouble by dreading tomorrow.
It is the dark menace of the future that makes cowards of us."*

— DOROTHY DAY

CHAPTER 11

Naming and Defeating Five Varieties of Worry

If you've ever faced a snarling stray dog, you've known fear. Simply say that dog's name, however, and the growling may stop, the ears drop, and the tail begin to wag. Knowing the dog's name gives you power over it.

God gave Adam the right to name all the animals. Naming implies dominion; the right to name confers power.

When Jesus went into the desert to fast and pray, the devil came to him and offered three temptations to deter him from his mission. Jesus faced his enemy, recognized him, and called him by name.

You need to face and name your enemies, the worries that plague you. To name them is to begin to exercise power over them.

Here are five common types of worry.

1) Info-ignorance

"A little knowledge is a dangerous thing," poet and philosopher Alexander Pope once noted. Sometimes, the more we know—or think we know—the more confused we become.

We read a lot about diseases and their prevention these days. A bulletin warns that a certain food causes cancer (at least in those poor, long-suffering lab rats). Another bulletin announces that a different food prevents cancer, or at least im-proves the odds of avoiding it. Next week, new studies will come out, and the foods may switch places on the "good for you/bad for you" lists.

In the 1950s, conscientious mothers were urged to serve their children a hearty, "balanced" breakfast of bacon and eggs, or perhaps pancakes slathered with syrup and butter, a big glass of whole milk on the side. Today many nutritionists find such a meal to be much too high in fat and calories and suggest whole grains, fruits, and skim milk instead.

Five varieties of worry— and how to combat them

1) Info-ignorance: Learn more and make a decision.

2) Future fear: Prepare fully and leave the rest to God.

3) Past tense: Decide to act, or decide not to act, and let it go.

4) Inertia: Engage in vigorous sloth-busting.

5) Evasion: Face the music— and remember who's leading the band.

As I write this, news reports warn of the imminent pandemic of so-called "bird flu." Commentators urge us to prepare —not always agreeing on how—even as they inform us that an effective vaccine may not be ready in time.

The barrage of information and misinformation can be awfully confusing, and it can promote and feed our anxieties.

2) Future fear

Next week you're scheduled to speak before a large group of strangers in a distant city you've never seen. It sounded like a wonderful opportunity when you made the commitment seven months ago, but now, with the confrontation only a few days away, you're becoming increasingly anxious.

You're not just worried about the speech. You're worried about getting to the airport on time, making your connecting flight, and finding your way around the strange city when you get there. You're also worried about your family's well-being while you're gone and about all the work that will pile up in your absence.

You're worried, in short, about a lot of things you can't do anything about yet. You can write and rehearse your speech now, but you can't take the trip yet.

3) Past tense

The more you think about it, the more you're certain that a casual remark you made to a friend last week hurt that friend's feelings. After all, she hasn't called, and she seems to be avoiding you.

You can try to apologize and explain that the remark was innocent, but that might only fan the flames. Deep down, you don't really think you have anything to apologize for, and even if you do say you're sorry, you can never unsay the remark.

Worry builds, and you feel completely powerless to do anything about it.

4) Inertia

You hate filing your income tax. All year you've thrown receipts, mileage slips, and other records into a desk drawer and forgotten about them. The tax forms are confusing and frustrating. You're not good with numbers. You fear that you're going to owe more money.

April 15 is drawing ever closer.

5) EVASION

If you take that great new job in a distant city, you'll be throwing away everything you've worked so hard for to get you where you are. You'll be leaving your friends behind, yanking your kids out of school, and saying good-bye to a home, a neighborhood, and a parish you love.

But you're in a rut at work, with no real hope for advancement. The new job offers stimulation, challenge, and considerably more money. You've visited the area and like it.

You list all the reasons to move in one column, all the reasons to stay in another. The scale seems to balance. Each choice promises big benefits; each carries a hefty price tag.

You put off making a decision. But you go right on worrying about it.

Take it to the Lord

"Come to me, all you that are weary and are carrying heavy burdens, and I will give you rest," Jesus assures us (Mt 11:28).

We've identified five varieties of worry; in dealing with them, each calls for a different approach. But in every case, the process begins with letting the Lord in on the dilemma. Define the problem as specifically as you can. Think about your options. (If you're using *The Worry Workbook* in conjunction with this text, you might want to try the "worry card" technique outlined there.)

Enter into God's presence. Praise and thank him, asking him to forgive your sins. Imagine Jesus, the Good Shepherd, bend-ing close to hear you, placing a hand on your shoulder. Tell him the problem. Alone, you may not be able to solve it, but with Jesus at your side, all things are possible.

Now you're ready to deal with specific worries in specific ways.

1) WISING UP TO INFO-IGNORANCE

"It ain't what we don't know that gets us in trouble," cowboy philosopher Will Rogers observed. "It's what we know for sure that ain't so."

A little knowledge may be dangerous, as Alexander Pope observed, but in the next line of the poem, he provides the cure. "Drink deeply," he advises, "or taste not" of the waters of knowledge.

Suppose you're concerned that you may not be eating healthy foods but are confused as to what to do about it. Commit yourself to finding out. Proper diet is worth more than a glance at the morning newspaper or casual attention to a story on the evening news. Newspapers like *The New York Times* and magazines like *American Health* publish the latest information in more depth and in plain English. Specialty magazines, like *Countdown,* the magazine of the Juvenile Diabetes Foundation, provide even more detail about their topics of interest.

Should you believe everything you see in print, even in more reliable sources? Of course not. But that doesn't mean you shouldn't read any of it. Quite the contrary. A more thorough study of a variety of sources can enable you to make sound decisions about vital questions, such as what you should be eating and drinking.

When you make those decisions, you'll banish the anxiety that stems from info-ignorance.

2) FORSAKING FUTURE FEAR

What can you do about that presentation you have to make next week? Prepare, check, and rehearse. Confirm your flight and hotel reservations. Work ahead as much as possible—without working yourself into a frenzy. Arrange to have contingencies covered while you're gone. Set a time when you'll call your family each night while you're away.

Stick to your regular routine as much as possible, including eating and sleeping patterns.

If worry floods you, review your preparations and remind yourself that you've done everything you can—and probably a lot more than you need to.

3) UNTENSING THE PAST

If there's something you can do about that uncaring remark you're afraid may have damaged a friendship, do it. Perhaps you can let go of your concern about who's right or wrong and simply apologize in Christian humility. You might be in for a happy surprise—a counter apology, a hug, an assurance that no offense was taken. Even if the result is less successful, you'll have acted, and that's critical here.

If there's truly nothing you can do, then decide, once and for all, that you will do nothing. Accept the consequences of your original action. When you start to worry, remind yourself, "I can do nothing," and move on.

You might even decide that you could do something but choose not to, preferring the situation as it is to the potential greater damage further action might create. Then decide you will do nothing; it's a valid decision.

Doesn't that leave you right back where you started? Far from it. The act of making a decision—and sticking with it—can free you or your anxiety. Decision brings peace.

4) Sloughing off sloth:
the cure for inertia

This solution is the simplest one in the book. It also may be the most difficult ("simple" does not mean "easy") and the most rewarding.

Terrified about the undone income tax? Do the income tax.

Use rewards (you get to do something wonderful when you're done). Anticipate the rush of relief and triumph you'll feel. Imagine the supreme joy of meeting the fear with a simple "All done" next time it surfaces. The Nike ad has it right. In many cases, the only thing to do is to just do it!

5) Avoiding evasion

This one may be considerably more complex. The decision to stay or move may be huge, the consequences potentially enormous. Your evasion may be rooted in anxieties that stretch back to childhood, when a move and change of schools traumatized you.

Think of all the major decisions you've made in your life: school, career, marriage (or other religious vocation)—the biggies. Did you have all the facts when you made those decisions? Could you foresee exactly where your decisions would lead you?

Of course not. You never can. As Robert Frost points out in his poem, "The Road Not Taken," you can't take both roads "and one traveler be," and you can't see very far down either road. Yet your choice will make "all the difference."

My wife, Ellen, son, Jeremiah, and I learned as much as we could about our potential move from Napa, California to Madison, Wisconsin. Would Ellen be productive and challenged intellectually and spiritually by the job she'd been offered with the Diocese of Madison? Could we make it all right on one paycheck if I didn't get a job right away? Would Jeremiah have a good school to go to? Would we survive the first time the temperature dropped below zero?

We also talked about what we were leaving. Most of our extended family lived in California. We had good jobs and good friends. We loved Napa. Jeremiah liked his school.

We submitted the decision to prayer—lots and lots of prayer. And then we jumped off the cliff and into the unknown. "And that has made all the difference."

Looking back, I can see God's hand in all of it. I can thank him for guiding us to this new land, new friends, new opportunities, new sorrow, and new growth. After twenty-seven years in Madison, I have some appreciation of just how little I knew about what that new life would be like and how much it would cost to claim it.

Consider this. In a fundamental sense, you can't make a "wrong" decision. Whatever you decide, asking for God's guidance and trusting in his love for you, you will grow in faith and love. You will find triumph and failure, sorrow and joy, because these are the essence of life on earth. You will more fully feel God's abiding and incredible love for you, and you will see more clearly his plan for your life.

When you look at it that way, just what are you worried about?

"Every evening I turn my worries over to God.
He's going to be up all night anyway."

— MARY C. CROWLEY

CHAPTER 12

How Are We to Pray?

If you're a parent, God has blessed you richly by letting you participate in the miracle of the creation of life. Raising these gifts from God, you experience the deepest joy and the sharpest pain life offers. You give your child your love, your time and energy, and your heart.

Your children become aware that they are separate from you and that they can say "no." They push you away, resent your corrections, protest your decisions, ignore your advice. This is as it must be. The child must struggle to become independent of the parent just as the chick must fight to break through the eggshell to be born. Often, the most difficult child becomes the most confident and capable adult.

You protect and teach your children, preparing them for the day when they'll go out into the world to make a life separate from you—far from your protection. You must prepare yourself to let go.

What if, after all your loving and caring and struggling, your child—now grown to be a man or woman—rejects your values? What if that young adult never writes, never visits, phones only to ask for help or money or to blame you when anything goes wrong? What would you say to such a child?

Would you ever stop loving that child?

Jesus taught us to call God "Father" ("Abba" translates more closely to "Daddy"). He demonstrated the Father's abiding love for us and called us to claim our heritage as God's children.

But aren't we sometimes like that ungrateful child? Don't we at times reject our Parent's teachings and "phone home" only when we want something, have a complaint, or want to cast blame for the messes we've gotten ourselves into?

God has given you life and everything you need to live that life abundantly in his Son. Every day you awaken to his new creation and the endless possibilities of life in the Spirit. God is present to you in every living thing.

Do you greet that day with prayers of gratitude?

Does God really want us to pray?

Catholics aren't alone in stressing the importance of daily prayer in the life of the faithful. Every major religion places a premium on prayer.

Islam teaches that prayer is the first duty Allah imposes, and Muslims will be held accountable on the Day of Judgment for their prayer habits. Prayer is a fundamental pillar of Islam, and failure to pray is considered a grievous sin.

Like Catholicism, Islam teaches that Allah has no need of our prayers. The act of praying is designed to help the one who prays.

Muslims believe that prayer strengthens and enlivens faith, purifies the heart, develops the mind, and cultivates the con-

science. Paralleling the Christian practice of the Liturgy of the
Hours, devout Muslims pause five times a day for obligatory
prayers of *Fajr, Dhuhr, Asr, Maghrib,* and *Isha*, beginning before
sunrise and ending when the sky is completely dark at night.

Judaism also stresses the centrality of daily prayer. Jews
believe that each day is holy and that they should seek reasons
to say 100 blessings a day. They believe they will be judged on
the performance of good works and daily rituals, such as
putting on the *Tallit* (prayer shawl) and *Tefillin* (or phylactery, a
small leather box containing verses from the Scriptures) to
pray three times a day. They must also observe strict dietary
laws. Ideally, prayers are recited in Hebrew, but Jews believe
that God understands them no matter what language they
employ—including silence in the presence of God. Jews
believe that prayer helps develop a right attitude and feeling, a
sharp mind and an understanding heart.

Praying must not be confined to moments of inspiration or
desperation. You don't simply pray when you feel like it. Prayer
should become second nature, as much a part of daily life as
breathing. Prayer is a discipline, to be pursued with diligence.
The observant Jew learns to pray through repetition.

"As a child learns to walk by walking," Rabbi Maurice
Lamm writes, "so we learn to pray by praying."[1]

There are special Jewish prayers for hearing thunder, notic-
ing the first bud of spring, and many other signs of God's power
and creation.

The most important of all Jewish prayers is the Shema,
which instructs Jews in how they are to live. The words will be
familiar to any Christian. They include the admonition, "You
shall love the Lord your God with all your heart, with all your
soul, and with all your might."

---

1. Rabbi Maurice Lamm, "Day-to-Day Judaism: Jewish prayer is a discipline.
Don't just wait for the mood to strike" (www.aish.com).

Although they acknowledge no specific "god out there" to whom they direct their thoughts, Buddhists also pray as a form of meditation, a tool in decision-making, and a path to awakening their inner strength and wisdom and the Great Compassion within them.

"Prayer is an important practice that serves to internalize the ideals of the Buddhist path," [2] writes Buddhist Senior Facilitator G. R. Lewis.

Prayer can "transform confusion into clarity and suffering into joy," Lewis writes. But to be effective, that prayer must be "devoid of self-centeredness and calculation, relying strictly on great compassion.... To benefit all beings." For the Buddhist, Lewis concludes, "prayer has nothing to do with begging for personal worldly or heavenly gains."

We can learn about prayer from all of these worldviews, but to know how we as Catholics are to pray, we must look to the teachings of the Christ.

"Master, teach us to pray"

My friend Jean Browman has a favorite prayer for the hard times. "Thank you, Lord, for the opportunity," she prays. "I sure hope you know what you're doing."

Note the use of "opportunity" for crisis and the willingness to thank God for the problem as being a part of the life he created for her.

Catholicism teaches that prayer should serve four key functions: to praise God, to thank God, to confess our sins, and to petition God for our needs. When the disciples asked Jesus to teach them how to pray, he gave us the beautifully simple and

---

2. G.R. Lewis, "Prayer in Buddhism" (www.buddhistfaith.tripod.com).

endlessly rich prayer we call the Lord's Prayer. Notice that it incorporates all four functions.

> "Our Father in heaven,
> hallowed be your name.
> Your kingdom come.
> Your will be done,
> on earth as it is in heaven.
> Give us this day our daily bread.
> And forgive us our debts,
> as we also have forgiven our debtors.
> And do not bring us to the time of trial,
> but rescue us from the evil one" (Mt 6:9–13).

We address God as our Father ("Abba/Daddy") and pay him homage. We ask that God's will, not our own, be done on earth. We ask for sustenance, forgiveness, and deliverance.

How many times have you prayed those words? Do you believe them? Do they still come from the heart?

To praise, to thank, to confess, and to petition.... How often we neglect the first three to stress only the fourth—our needs of the moment.

As children, we may pray to "Santa God," who "knows when we've been bad or good" and dispenses punishments or rewards as our conduct merits. But what happens when we pray to Santa God, and he doesn't deliver? What if we say our prayers and mind our parents, drink our milk and clean our plates, and we still don't get the new bicycle or the baby brother or the passing grade on the math test?

What does Santa God do when players on both teams pray fervently for victory? Does the team with the better prayers, rather than players, win?

Many of us were disillusioned when we first learned that Daddy and Mommy were really Santa Claus and that the jolly old man existed in myth and spirit only. Some stop praying to Santa God soon thereafter. Unfortunately, some stop praying altogether. If I don't get a pony under the Christmas tree, what's the point?

Didn't Jesus teach us to ask and we shall be answered, seek and we shall find, knock and the door shall be opened unto us? He did. We may forget, though, that this admonition comes right after he taught us to pray that God's will be done. That's the prayer that will surely be answered for us. Our quest to know God better and love him more fully will be successful if we persevere, and this is all we ever really need, the only thing of real worth in this world or the world to come.

Using prayer to solve problems

Oh, I get it, the cynic might say. *God will always answer our prayers as long as we always pray for what he wants to give us anyway.*

It might seem that way to the cynic—and to the cynical element in each of us. But then, a cynic can never trust enough to begin living in faith, and we must *live* our faith, rather than trying to understand or analyze or "prove" it. That's not to say, however, that prayer is ultimately "useless" in the earthly sense.

I first heard of the "dynamics of prayer for solving problems" from Keith James, who was living in Scottsdale Tasmania, Australia. He attributed it to Shoghi Effendi. Here's the four-step process as Keith outlined it to me:

Step 1:   *Pray and meditate on the problem, and then "remain in the silence of contemplation" for a few minutes.*

In other words, stop talking and just listen. Let silence fill you. It isn't easy, at least not for me. Self-consciousness (what writer Natalie Goldberg calls "monkey mind") rushes in to fill the void with chatter. You must corral the monkey and gently dismiss it, inviting the silence back. Don't strain to hear. Just listen.

You may, indeed, be communicating with God in ways too deep for consciousness. "...The Spirit helps us in our weakness," Paul tells us, "for we do not know how to pray as we ought, but that very Spirit intercedes with sighs too deep for words" (Rom 8:26).

But isn't that mere meditation under the guise of prayer?

First, there's nothing "mere" about meditation. It's a difficult discipline to master and a great aid in combating the noise and hyperactivity of our times.

Second, we aren't "only" meditating. We're placing ourselves in the Father's presence, seeking his will for us.

Step 2:   *Have faith and confidence that the Spirit will flow through you, the right way will reveal itself, the door will open.*

"Fear is useless," Jesus told the father of the little girl he thought had died. "What is needed is trust" (cf. Mk 5:36).

You *will* receive an answer. It might not come immediately. Be patient. Repeat your petition often. When an answer does come, it may be as soft as that "still, small voice," a gentle soul-stirring. You'll recognize it as being from God if it's consistent with God's teachings.

Remember, too, that "no" and "not yet" are also answers. In his perfect love, the Father gives his children what we *need* on the journey of the soul. You may not understand, agree with, or appreciate the answer at the time. You will perhaps understand only when you see God face to face in the next life.

Step 3:   *Before you rise from your prayer, linger silently in God's presence, thanking him for hearing and answering your prayer. As you reenter the world, act as if your prayer has been answered. Be mindful of God's power, and trust that he will act through you.*

Step 4:   *When you feel that you've received your answer,*
             act on it.

If a decision or solution truly seems to have come in
response to your prayer, carry it out. This is not a wish but
rather a resolution, a specific act you will perform the first time
it's possible to do so.

The role of ritual prayer

We often petition God spontaneously, especially when we
feel most helpless and in need, and we pray in our own words.

There's a place, too, for ritualistic and rote prayers.

I began attending daily Mass almost two decades ago.
Anxiety drove me to the student chapel two blocks from my
office each noon. I felt powerless to solve my problems and
to help those I love most. I needed assistance, spiritually and
emotionally, and I figured a form of worship my Church has
prescribed for over two millennia might help and certainly
couldn't hurt.

At first I often felt as if I were going through the motions.
My mind constantly wandered. I wondered if I might be doing
more harm than good and looked for reasons to excuse myself
from the "obligation" I was imposing on myself.

Something—I would now identify it as the Spirit—kept
drawing me back, even though for a long time all that "extra"
praying didn't seem to be helping. About the only good I could
claim from the process was a feeling that I had done the right
thing when I was finished, and that good feeling often devolved
into smug self-righteousness.

Mass gradually became a habit. I stopped fighting about
whether I'd go or not and just started going, no matter how I
felt about it.

Gradually—over months and even years of repetition—attending Mass stopped being difficult. Time spent in communal prayer began to flow by swiftly. Often I lost track of time and stopped thinking about the demands awaiting me. I began to feel a spiritual renewal, even, or perhaps especially, on the bad days.

Now I look forward to Mass as an opportunity to join my faith community in prayer, to be strengthened and lifted up, to be present to them as they are present to me. It isn't an obligation any more. It's an opportunity, and I feel deprived when I can't attend.

Perhaps a dozen years ago I began staying after Mass on Friday to pray the Rosary. It was as if I were starting the process all over again. The prayers were almost painful and seemed to take forever. Again the process was gradual—submission to the habit, a sense of ease and purpose, and finally a spiritual renewal.

I don't quite look forward to the Rosary—yet—but I suspect that will come with time.

After Mass, I return to the daily "wars" much better able to hang onto the rock of my salvation through the most violent storms. I have begun to receive and accept the rich spiritual blessings God has for us whenever two or more gather in his name.

Other examples of ritual prayer, either communal or solitary, might include a simple prayer of thanksgiving and praise on awakening, observance of the Liturgy of the Hours, a blessing over meals, prayers for the saints' intercession on their feast days, and prayer before sleeping.

If words fail you at such times, simply rely on the only prayer we ever really need, the one our Savior and Brother Jesus gave us, the Lord's Prayer.

> *"...Do you not know that your body is a temple*
> *of the Holy Spirit within you, which you have from God,*
> *and that you are not your own?"*
>
> — 1 CORINTHIANS 6:19

CHAPTER 13

Maintaining the Temple of the Spirit

Biking home from work the other day, I spied a bumper sticker that has stayed with me: *"We are spiritual beings having a physical experience."*

Some consider the body to be the anchor of the soul and death to be liberation from the burden of the flesh. Maybe so, but God gave us our bodies and put us here on earth, subject to the physical laws he established for it. Finding physical harmony in nature is an important part of our spirit-journey.

Keeping physically fit should be part of your spiritual exercise routine. If you want to draw closer to God and experience the rich blessing of spiritual peace, you mustn't ignore the proper care and feeding of your body, which is the temple of your soul.

Yet fewer and fewer of us seem to be taking the care we should of the bodies God has given us. Examining just one aspect of physical fitness, maintaining a healthy weight, provides startling evidence of the decline in fitness over the last fifteen years.

According to statistics compiled by an outfit called the American Obesity Association (itself an ominous modern phenomenon), the incidence of overweight Americans (a body mass index or BMI above 25) rose from 56 percent in 1994 to 64.5 percent in 2000. That means that, according to the AOA, anyway, almost two-thirds of us are overweight—not as judged by supermodel stick-figure standards, but by a scientific guideline.

In the same period, the percentage of obese Americans (BMI over 30) rose from 23 to 30.5 percent, and the severely obese (BMI above 40) rose from 2.9 to 4.7 percent.

According to the Centers for Disease Control and Prevention (CDC), a BMI of 30 generally means that the bearer is about thirty pounds overweight. The CDC, an organization with no particular stake in proclaiming obesity to be a problem, provides statistics that confirm the dire findings of the AOA. In the decade of the 1990s, their figures show, obesity among adults in America increased by nearly 60.[1]

Statistics for children are similar—and similarly ominous.

Is being overweight harmful to your health? Apart from fashion considerations and "Big is beautiful" movements, extra weight puts more strain on the joints. The heart must work harder to supply blood to all those new cells. Try carrying a thirty-pound sack of kitty litter any appreciable distance and experience the difference being overweight makes to your stamina.

Again, CDC statistics confirm what common sense tells us. Physical inactivity and being overweight account for more than

---

1. The most current health statistics are available on the website for the Center for Disease Control: http://www.cdc.gov/nchs/hus.htm.

300,000 premature deaths a year in America, making fat cells the second leading killer behind tobacco. Studies also confirm a causal link between weight and the onset of diabetes, which increased by 33 percent among American adults during the 1990s, again according to CDC statistics.

Obesity is more prevalent among men than women, but not by much. It seems to peak in the decade of life between fifty-five and sixty-four years of age, and then decline slightly. The more education we have, the less likely we are to be obese. Folks in the South tend to weigh more than New Englanders.[2]

How did we get so fat?

We eat too much and move too little. When our bodies cry out for rest or crave physical activity, we give them sugar and caffeine instead.

Even if we consciously try to cut the fat and calories in our diets, we may become confused and misled by "low-fat" and "lite" labels. The Food and Drug Administration (FDA) now defines "low-fat" as a food containing three grams or less per serving. Is that good or bad? Compared to what? And are those all "bad" fats or the alleged "good" kind? "Low-calorie" means forty calories or fewer per serving. But nothing stops the food manufacturer from deciding that a small bag of chips, the kind we wolf down in minutes, actually contains six "servings."

We may mistakenly think a "low-fat" food therefore contains relatively few calories, which isn't necessarily the case.

And we put our faith in fad diets such as the "low-carb" mania (now dying out, thank heavens), which prescribed eating

---

2. For figures on comparative levels of obesity by region, see www.wrong diagnosis.com. These statistics are based on the 2004 U.S. Census Bureau. For more information, see Nancy Hellmich, "Obesity in America is worse than ever" (*USA TODAY*, October 9, 2006).

as much protein and fat as you could hold, as long as you avoided breads and grains! Intuitively, doesn't that just seem crazy?

A friend of mine went on the "diet of nines." On this ingenious regimen, you eat nine bananas on day one—and nothing else. The next day you get nine eggs—and only nine eggs. The third day calls for, believe it or not, nine hot dogs—no buns. If you're still alive and not completely demented after that, you're supposed to start the cycle over, but it's hard to imagine anyone lasting longer than three days eating like that anyway.

Food and drink aren't the only factors in our assault on our own bodies, of course. When we're anxious and stressed, we self-medicate with nicotine and alcohol or "ask our doctor" about some pill that promises to bliss us out—instead of bringing our fears to our loving Father.

What should we do about it?

Just as God gave us the Ten Commandments as a guide to right living and spiritual well-being rather than a set of rules to be followed "or else," guidelines for eating right and getting proper exercise and rest aren't odious rules designed to make our lives miserable. They're a blueprint for physical well-being—and part of spiritual good health as well.

And just as he does with the Ten Commandments, so God gives us free will to follow or ignore these guidelines. Failure to obey brings its own punishment—spiritual pain and degradation in the case of violating the Commandments, deteriorating health in the case of physical "laws."

Experts disagree over how to interpret the laws of nature as they seem to govern our bodies. Dietary guidelines have shifted radically over the years, so much so that even the sacrosanct "Food Pyramid," long our government's standard for healthy eating, has given way to a variety of new pyramids.

When I first began exercising regularly, "experts" preached the doctrine of "no pain, no gain"; we were to push ourselves beyond fatigue and even pain in order to achieve fitness. Then the pendulum swung the other way, and we were assured that "any exercise is better than no exercise." Even long-despised housework began to count as a calorie-burning, muscle-toning workout.

Now we seem to be seeking a middle ground, with experts recommending thirty minutes or more of "moderate" exercise five days a week. (Now let the debate begin about what constitutes "moderate" exercise.) So, what should you do?

Clearly, "supersizing" food and drink portions and spending increasing amounts of time sitting in front of a television and computer aren't getting the job done.

You consume calories in the form of food and drink. You burn calories in the form of exercise. Some foods are much denser in calories than others. (Compare a triple bacon cheeseburger with a soy burger.) Some exercises burn many more calories than others (running seven miles in forty-nine minutes as opposed to giving the thumb a workout channel surfing the television, for example).

Living the wisdom of Satchel Paige

I've already quoted Satchel Paige, who may have been the greatest baseball pitcher who ever lived. We'll never know for sure, since the barrier erected by racial prejudice kept Paige from pitching in the whites-only Major Leagues until he was already well past his prime. But his performances in the professional Negro Leagues and in barnstorming exhibitions against black and white teams, along with anecdotal evidence from teammates like Buck O'Neill, provide ample testimony to his greatness.

Paige kept pitching, day after day, year after year, traveling from town to town and game to game in old cars on bad roads, often sleeping in those cars when no hotel in town would accommodate him and his black teammates. He didn't have the benefit of modern sports medicine. No trainer accompanied him.

He certainly didn't live a Spartan life, but old Satch had been given incredible talent, remarkable endurance, and an indomitable spirit, and he learned how to listen to his body and give it what it needed.

"Avoid fried food, which anger up the blood," he advised decades ago in his *Rules for Right Living.* "If your stomach disputes you, lie down and pacify it with cooling thoughts. Keep the juice flowing by jangling around gently as you move. Go lightly on vices such as carrying on in society—the social ramble ain't restful."

Still good advice.

Here's a quick rundown of what the burgeoning science of diet and nutrition and the field of sports physiology have added to Paige's intuitions.

Ten moderate, common-sense guidelines for diet and exercise

1) Include lots of fresh fruits, veggies, and whole grains in your diet.

2) Avoid fats and processed sugars in excess.

3) Don't take in more calories than you burn (or you'll store the excess as fat).

Ellen has all kinds of tricks for cutting down on fats and calories—substituting low-fat yogurt for mayonnaise in her famous "spinach surprise," for example.

Dr. Art Ulene gave a demonstration on *The Today Show* in which he presented two seemingly identical sets of meals, one made with conventional in-gredients, the other with low- or non-fat substitutes. The first three meals con-tained 2,300 calories (not a bad daily intake for an active adult), but 55 percent of those calories were derived from fat—not so good for anybody. The seemingly id-entical meals made with the substitutes contained only 1,200 calo-ries, and only 7 percent of those calories came from fat.

4) Graze rather than stuff, that is, eat smaller amounts several times a day rather than one or two huge meals.

This sort of "grazing" aids digestion and helps the body absorb and use the nutrients in the food you eat. You also feel less hungry and experi-ence fewer of those food cravings that have destroyed many a diet.

5) Dine at breakfast, but snack at dinner.

The Irish seem to have the right idea with their le-

Ten Guidelines for Healthy Living

1) Include lots of fresh fruits, veggies, and whole grains in your diet.

2) Avoid fats and processed sugars in excess.

3) Don't take in more calories than you burn (or you'll store the excess as fat).

4) Graze rather than stuff.

5) Dine at breakfast, but snack at dinner.

6) Don't eat anything substantial within two hours of bedtime.

7) Find some form of exercise that's right for you.

8) Make exercise a habit.

9) Avoid heavy exercise within two or three hours of bedtime.

10) Eliminate nicotine, and use caffeine and alcohol in moderation.

gendary "full Irish" breakfast. It's huge! The downside is that it includes at least two and often three forms of pork.

It's best to eat the big meal soon after getting up, when your need for fuel is highest, and taper off until bedtime. Most of us do just the opposite, skimping on or even skipping breakfast (but grabbing two donuts at the office?) and eating a big dinner.

6) Don't eat anything substantial within two hours of bedtime.

Digestion is an extremely active process and can disrupt sleep.

7) Find some form of exercise that's right for you.

Explore moderate forms of exercise that tone rather than tear down. Seek activities you enjoy (and are thus more apt to perform). Exercise at least a little each day rather than sitting all week and trying to get in a mega-workout on Saturday, which will be unpleasant and can cause you to hurt yourself and give up exercising altogether.

8) Make exercise a habit.

Eliminate all debate. It's *so* easy to rationalize not exercising at any given moment, and those moments add up to an inactive life. Exercise at about the same time every day.

9) As with eating, avoid heavy exercise within two or three hours of bedtime.

Exercise elevates your heart rate and metabolism. That's great for conditioning and weight maintenance but not so good for sleeping.

10) Eliminate nicotine, and use caffeine and alcohol in moderation.

I quit smoking when my son was born thirty-seven years ago. About fifteen years ago I decided I'd already drunk my quota of alcohol and quit that, too.

Caffeine remains my drug of choice, and some days I over-do it.

If I had my druthers, everyone would quit tobacco and alcohol. Along with being disgusting, smoking kills you (and possibly those around you). I can't say as I've ever known alcohol to do anybody any good, and I've certainly seen it do a lot of folks great harm—physically, mentally, and spiritually.

Caffeine is an acceptable drug in our culture, and recent studies seem to exonerate it of all health crimes except from being addictive (highly so). But we need to respect it as the powerful stimulant it is. If hyper tension, nervousness, or sleeplessness is a problem for you, tapering off on caffeine couldn't hurt.

But aren't we doing all that stuff anyway?

It's hard to pick up a magazine or lifestyle section of the newspaper these days without encountering advice on exercise and diet. All that good talk about good health might lead us to believe that, as a nation, we've become quite health-conscious. But the article on "ten tasty ways to use tofu on your Thanksgiving table" will be surrounded by ads for all the tasty, fattening stuff and recipes for making them ever tastier and more fattening.

We talk good diet and exercise, but we let Jane Fonda and Richard Simmons get our exercise for us. If you decide to amend your eating habits and work exercise into your daily routine, you'll find yourself bucking considerable societal pressure.

You'll also have to battle your own habit patterns. Those habits are very hard to break, especially when they get tangled up with emotional needs, as diet and exercise often do. "The spirit indeed is willing, but the flesh is weak" (Mt 26:41).

You'll also no doubt find it difficult to add a new activity to your already overfilled life. You'll never find time to exercise. You'll have to *make* the time. Schedule your workout sessions, and honor your commitment to them. Know that if you use thirty minutes to exercise, you'll have to take that thirty minutes from some other activity. Make a conscious decision about what you're giving up, or else you'll take the time from sleep and relationships by default.

Be gentle, patient, and persistent with yourself. Keep working at it. Listen to your body, and bring your doubts and concerns to your loving Father.

> *"When they take you before...rulers and the authorities,*
> *do not worry about how you are to defend yourselves*
> *or what you are to say; for the Holy Spirit will teach you*
> *at that very hour what you ought to say."*
>
> — Luke 12:11–12

CHAPTER 14

Five Ways to Get Worry to Work for You

Suppose you have to give a speech to several hundred strangers. Does the thought make your palms sweat and your throat dry up? If so, you're not alone. Opinion polls reveal that public speaking is the number-one fear among Americans. We fear it more than illness, more than poverty, even more than death.

So I've selected America's number-one fear to illustrate five important principles for getting worry to worry for you.

Step 1: *Replace worry with work.*

Preparation can defuse much of your anxiety. For that hypothetical speech, research thoroughly, as well in advance of the speech as possible, and write a complete outline. The very fact that you're acting will do much to alleviate your fear. Then rehearse diligently—in front of the mirror, your dog, or a sympathetic friend.

When the speech flows smoothly, rehearse it three more times.

Step 2:   *Visualize success.*

As the time of the speech approaches, disaster movies may begin playing in the theater of your mind. Now showing in your poor, fevered brain: "Speaker makes idiot of self; audience riots in protest."

Cancel that unfortunate booking. Instead, imagine yourself giving your speech fluently, with your audience listening attentively. The name of your movie should be: "Brilliant speaker has rapt audience hanging on every word."

Step 3:   *Get out of the way.*

Not all of you is afraid—only the self-conscious ego self, which worries constantly about what others think of you. Gently tell your poor, frightened ego, *"This isn't about you."* Concentrate on what you want to say. Think about what the listeners have come to hear. What will they get for spending their precious time listening to you? How will your talk make their lives better?

When your ego again cries for attention, gently tell it once more: *"This isn't about you."* Continue to focus on your message and on your listeners' needs. In other words, put yourself third here and all of them second.

God, of course, comes first.

Step 4:   *Ask for God's guidance.*

Every time I'm privileged to give a talk, lead a workshop, or proclaim the Word at Mass, I recite the end of Psalm 19: "Let the words of my mouth and the meditation of my heart be acceptable to you, O LORD, my rock and my redeemer" (19:14).

I started doing this after reading that one of my heroes, legendary sportscaster Red Barber, always used this simple prayer before going on the air.

It has never let me down.

Step 5:   *Understand that your audience wants you to succeed.*

Do you go to Mass hoping that the sermon will be tedious? Of course not. You want the priest to succeed, because you want to be informed, enriched, perhaps even inspired by his words.

Most people in your audience will feel the same way about you. They didn't come to hear a bad talk. They came to hear a good one. They're pulling for you. And most will assume that you know what you're talking about until and unless you prove otherwise.

Five Steps to Combat Fear of public speaking— or any other fear

1) Replace worry with work.

2) Visualize success.

3) Get out of the way.

4) Ask for God's guidance.

5) Understand that your audience wants you to succeed.

Fear is a choice

You can choose not to worry—about giving a speech or any other fear-evoking task. But you have to work at it.

You can choose to become more physically fit, for example—but it will require dedication of time and energy and the discipline to keep working at it, especially in the beginning, when it doesn't feel good or come naturally.

It's the same with praying, speaking in public, shooting a basket, or cooking a meal. The more you work at it, the better you get—and the less you worry.

Once you choose not to worry, you will begin to reclaim your life, gradually releasing energy and joy you'd forgotten you had. You'll also be a better public speaker—or whatever else you set your mind to do.

Of course you'll still worry the first several (dozen?) times. Prepare, rehearse, visualize, and pray. When anxiety comes, welcome it as a sign that you're alive and properly stimulated by the opportunity before you. Stop worrying about worrying. We all do it. Take a deep, cleansing breath. Stop thinking about you and start thinking about them. Gently lead yourself back into the presence of God.

"I sought the LORD, and he answered me, and delivered me from all my fears" (Ps 34:4).

If your mind continues to insist on showing disaster films, patiently change the reel and cue up the new success feature.

Your ego is like a frightened child: alone, bewildered, and terrified of vague shadows and strange noises. Embrace that poor child, as you would your own frightened son or daughter. Tell that child, "Don't be afraid. I'll take care of you."

Then listen to your loving Father, who is telling you the same thing.

Case study: On the next Oprah...

"Hi. My name is Angie, and I'm calling for the *Oprah Show*." God had just called my bluff.

I teach workshops on writing and publishing. When we talk about ways authors can help promote their books, including participating on talk shows, I often used to joke that "Oprah hasn't called me yet, but when she does, I'll be ready."

Now Oprah—or one of her assistant producers, anyway—was calling. Was I ready?

"We're doing a program on 'how to avoid losing your cool,'" Angie told me. "We want you to be one of our guest experts."

"When?" I managed, figuring they arranged these things months in advance.

"Next Tuesday. Would you be available?"

"Yes. I'd be available next Tuesday," said a voice sounding something like mine, only squeakier.

Somebody with the show had read a book I'd written on stress management, *Slow Down—and yet more done*. The producers apparently felt that this little book qualified me as a national expert on stress. I wrote the book because I needed it—the same reason I wrote this one.

I'd done a lot of radio interviews, been on local television, and on cable television in Sheboygan. So facing a camera and a microphone wouldn't be new to me.

But Oprah!

Angie and her cohorts left little to chance, calling several times a day to go over my segments of the show. I was also plenty busy with my teaching and writing.

I was on the Interstate, bound for Chicago, when it suddenly occurred to me that Oprah's audience was considerably bigger than the one in Sheboygan.

I started breathing deeply—breathing is always good when panic strikes—and felt myself hyperventilating.

"Thank you for the opportunity, Lord," I prayed. "I sure hope you know what we're doing."

The panic passed. It always does. But every time the word "Oprah" flashed through my consciousness, my stomach took a rueful tumble. As I drove into nightfall and the suburbs of Chicago, I couldn't remember any of the points Angie had discussed with me. *What if I went blank while on camera?*

See what I mean about God calling my bluff? Here was a wonderful opportunity to practice what I preach about conquering anxiety.

I checked in at the "All-Suites Omni" (where we TV stars stay), had dinner, took a walk. Back in my suite, I took out one of my oversized yellow note cards and a magic marker and boiled my presentation down to four or five key reminder words. I studied the list, covered it, recited it. I rehearsed various ways of phrasing my suggestions—without trying to memorize specific sentences. I visualized myself smiling and confident, trading quips with Oprah while the audience laughed and applauded.

Then I prayed that God would cleanse my spirit, guide my steps, and give me the serenity and the words I'd need.

I managed to fall asleep but awoke well before dawn. Then again, I always do. I hadn't closed the curtains, not wanting to miss a thing, and the lights of Chicago glistened outside my window. I prayed, studied my card, rehearsed my points, went for my daily jog. As I trotted down fabled Michigan Avenue, I rehearsed some more.

By the time the limo picked me up (oh, yes! A limo!) to take me to the studios of Harpo Productions, I had, no doubt, grossly over-prepared. That's okay. For Oprah, you over-prepare!

While I waited in the green room (green is supposed to be soothing) until it was time to appear on stage, I chatted with the show's makeup man. I could hear the audience laugh and applaud just down the hall and on the television monitor above my head. The show I was hearing was actually happening just a few feet away!

An associate producer beckoned. My moment in the spotlight was at hand.

A strange and wonderful thing happened.

The stage was a theater in the round, an open ring surrounded by bleachers full of folks (not as many as it looks like on television, but plenty). The young lady led me to my chair, across the stage from…Oprah herself, working with a panel of some of the self-professed most impatient and stressed-out people in the world talking about how they cut in line at movies and run red lights.

I listened intently, becoming absorbed in their stories. I became especially concerned for a woman named Marlene, who described how she had once nearly injured one of her children when she picked up the child at school. In her impatience, she had pulled away from the curb before the child had gotten all the way into the van, and the poor kid had had to cling to the door for dear life. The audience roared, as if she'd told a great joke. Marlene laughed with them, but I thought she looked sad beneath the forced smile.

As I thought about Marlene and her life of hyper-stress, I stopped thinking about me and my anxiety.

We went into commercial break, and another associate producer led me to center stage and sat me in a chair near Oprah, who stood, microphone in hand, waiting for her cue.

My heart pounded, but I was hardly aware of my body. I said a final silent prayer as I watched the words of my introduction on the teleprompter across from me and simultaneously heard Oprah speak the words. She called me a "recovering speedaholic"—one of the phrases I'd used in my bio for the book.

I took a deep, centering breath. Time seemed to slow. Calm came over me. I remembered all the points I was supposed to make—and decided not to make them. Instead, I turned to Marlene, smiled, and began to talk to her.

I don't remember exactly what I said, but it was probably something like, "We're always in such a hurry to get to the next place. But life isn't about getting to the next place. Life is right here, right now."

Marlene smiled and nodded. Oprah asked me some questions. I might even have mentioned some of the points I'd discussed ahead of time.

We went into another commercial break. I wondered if all those associate producers would attack me for not sticking to the script. I glanced at Oprah, who didn't look at all concerned. She nodded and mouthed the words, "Nice job." (I think she did, anyway. It's hard to believe now.)

The next two segments flew by. I was actually enjoying myself.

"We're running a little short," one of the assistants whispered, having materialized at my shoulder. "She might toss it back to you for some final tips."

I looked up at one of the teleprompters (they're everywhere) and watched the lettering spell out, "MARSHALL ARE THERE ANY FINAL TIPS YOU'D LIKE TO GIVE US?" As I finished reading, I heard Oprah saying, "Marshall, are there any final tips you'd like to give us?"

That's me she's talking to!

I think I gave her my tip about taking four vacations every day to break the stress cycle. Folks applauded. The lights over the cameras went out. Another assistant led me back to the green room.

My stint on national television was over—except for reruns.

Marlene came in as I was gathering up my hat and my "Oprah Show" coffee mug.

"Are you really a 'recovering speedaholic'?" she asked, looking at me intently.

"Yeah. Accent on the recover*ing.*"

She smiled, nodded. "Then maybe there's hope for me," she said.

And then I knew for sure what God was teaching me that day. My big moment with Oprah wasn't about me. It was about Marlene—and anybody else who might have heard something that would help them to slow down and reclaim their lives.

All that remained for me was to thank him, praise him, and try never to forget this wonderful teaching.

"Love your enemies, do good to those who hate you."

— LUKE 6:27

CHAPTER 15

Don't Get Mad. Don't Get Even. Get Peaceful.

My father was a powerful, athletic man all his life, and he had a strong temper. But as he grew older, he became more and more at peace with the world. As his body failed, his spirit grew stronger. In his last days before he died of cancer, I spent a lot of time at his bedside. One morning, he said something I'll carry with me always.

"I used to get so mad at people," he reflected. "Now I just say a little prayer for them."

While dying on the cross, Jesus prayed that the Father would forgive his tormenters. Can you imagine? Even in his agony, he sought salvation for his killers, a final, astounding act of forgiveness.

He had always preached forgiveness, of course, stressing in parables that God would deal with us precisely as we dealt with others. Think of the foolish servant, whose master forgives him a huge debt, but who then refuses to forgive a much smaller one. When the master finds out, he has the perfidious servant cast into jail. So it will be for us, Jesus warned, if we fail to forgive.

How many times are we to forgive? Not seven, but seventy times seven, which was his way of saying always.

Imagine what the world would be like if we actually lived by this precept. The divorce rate would plunge. Crimes of vengeance would vanish. Spite fences, literal and figurative, would come tumbling down. Peace and harmony would reign. The lion would lie down with the lamb. God's will would truly be done "on earth, as it is in heaven."

You'll probably never be called on to endure the kind of suffering Christ accepted for us. But you may have experienced heartbreak in love and betrayal in the workplace. You've probably been the victim of at least one crime. You encounter aggravations, slights, and offenses every day of your life. Just trying to unwind and relax at the movies can become an exercise in anger management.

An idiot cuts you off in traffic on the way to the theater, causing you to brake so hard your neck aches for a week. Another idiot slips into "your" parking space at the mall. When you finally find a place to park, you discover that still another idiot has dumped a mound of stale cigarette butts on the ground for you to step in. Some cretin sitting behind you in the theater talks constantly through the movie.

You leave the theater more uptight than when you arrived —and then still another idiot driver takes so long making a left turn on the arrow, she makes you miss the signal.

Forgive? Maybe later. First you have to teach that bozo a lesson. So you honk your horn, yell, and shake your fist. It may not do any good, but at least you feel better, right?

Wrong. By venting your anger, you actually feed it. The act of yelling alerts your body that you're in danger, and it pumps even more adrenaline into your system, preparing you for the battle to come. You turn a mild upset into a much bigger one.

God doesn't tell us to forgive just so we can be good people; he's giving us practical advice in healthy living for our own good. When we forgive, we are healed of our anger.

There's another bad outcome when you yell at that inattentive driver. He becomes as enraged at you as you were at him, ready to yell at the next person who gets in his way. Anger spreads like a contagion.

You may have succeeded in punishing the driver, putting a hot poker in his guts, just like the one you're carrying around in yours. But punishment isn't your job. It's God's. "Do not look for revenge...for it is written, 'Vengeance is mine, I will repay, says the Lord'" (Rom 12:19).

Defusing the bomb before it explodes

I always assumed that anger was a force of nature, an inevitable and even healthy reaction, and that trying to stifle anger is harmful, like stifling a sneeze. Yelling when I'm mad seemed as natural as smiling when I'm happy. I've discovered that I get to choose what to do with my anger.

When the adrenaline surge hits, I can let it sweep me into noisy confrontation, or I can take a deep breath, pray, and remind myself that Christ is in the other, just as he is in me. On a good day, I can even laugh at myself for getting so upset. On a really good day, I remember to ask God to bless the fellow who nearly ran me off the road.

When I do, my body relaxes and my spirit grows calm. Instead of paroxysms, I get peace. The more times I experience this peace, the more natural it feels and the faster the adrenaline surge subsides.

Sometimes—and this seems truly miraculous to me—when I replace the curse with a blessing, I don't even get the jolt of adrenaline at all.

Defusing the rage response has been a long, slow process, requiring much prayer, patience, and practice. When I'm tired or in a hurry (I'm frequently both), I sometimes slide back into the old anger pattern. But I succeed more often than I fail; and if I can do it, so can you.

A student in one of my stress management seminars taught me an even better way to handle the parking-lot-ashtray-dump vexation. She carries a hand broom, a dustpan, and a paper bag in the car with her at all times. When she finds a mess, she simply gets out the clean-up kit and takes care of it herself.

That's not fair, you protest. She didn't make the mess, so why should she have to clean it up? You're right. It isn't fair. And she didn't have to clean it up. She chose to. That makes all the difference. By doing so, she got rid of the offensive filth and got to feel good about herself, all for a few seconds of sweeping.

On one such occasion, she told us, as she bent to her self-appointed chore, she heard someone walk up behind her.

"Sorry," a man's voice said. "I wasn't thinking. Let me."

The man took the broom and dustpan from her and cleaned up after himself.

Then they both drove away feeling good. That sounds a lot better to me than fuming about the mess and leaving it to discourage and anger others.

We are called not just to tolerate but to love

Jesus asks us for more than mere civility, more than grudging tolerance. He calls us to love our enemies and to do good to those who hate us.

"…Bless those who curse you, pray for those who abuse you. If anyone strikes you on the cheek, offer the other also; and from anyone who takes away your coat do not withhold even your shirt. Give to everyone who begs from you; and if anyone takes away your goods, do not ask for them again" (Lk 6:28–30).

That's a tall order!

I grew up wanting to be a real man, like John Wayne. In his last movie, *The Shootist,* his character, J. B. Books, expresses the credo that many of the Duke's characters lived by: "I won't be wronged, I won't be insulted, and I won't be laid a hand on."

Hit me and I'll hit you back—harder, if I can.

As I grew older, I tried to reconcile John Wayne with Jesus Christ, but in the end, I couldn't meld revenge and forgiveness into a workable compromise. For the follower of Christ, there is just no escaping "Do to others as you would have them do to you" (Lk 6:31) or "Bless those who persecute you; bless and do not curse them" (Rom 12:14).

That Scripture continues:

Do not repay anyone evil for evil, but take thought for what is noble in the sight of all. If it is possible, so far as it depends on you, live peaceably with all. Beloved, never avenge yourselves…. Do not be overcome by evil, but overcome evil with good (12:17–19, 21).

It's not enough to refrain from hitting our brothers and sisters. We can't even passively hate them. We must love them.

Listen to these words from 1 John 2:10–11:

Whoever loves a brother or sister lives in the light, and in such a person there is no cause for stumbling. But whoever hates another believer is in the darkness, walks in the darkness, and does not know the way to go, because the darkness has brought on blindness.

Again in 1 John 3:14–15 we read:

> Whoever does not love abides in death. All who hate a brother or sister are murderers, and you know that murderers do not have eternal life abiding in them.

We may not feel like loving a person who wrongs us. But love is an action, not a feeling. We are called to act with love. This is the higher way, the way of Jesus, the way of peace and light.

*"Real difficulties can be overcome.
It is only the imaginary ones that are unconquerable."*

—THEODORE N. VAIL

CHAPTER 16

Seeking Mercy Instead of Justice

Rabbi Harold Kushner had a runaway bestseller a few years back with *When Bad Things Happen to Good People*.

Our sense of justice is outraged when evil befalls someone we consider to be a good person. It's especially outraged when that person happens to be us! Do people deserve what they get?

When Hurricane Katrina struck the Gulf Coast, leveling huge parts of New Orleans, some were quick to say that the city's wide-open lifestyle had brought about its devastation. They saw in "The Big Easy" a modern-day Sodom and Gomorrah. This sort of "blaming the victim" is judgmental and wrong.

We want to believe that good is rewarded and evil punished in this world. But even casual observation reveals that evil seems at times to prosper, while the just are struck down by illness and disaster.

Shouldn't a loving, just, and all-powerful God reward good and punish evil? And if he doesn't, must we conclude that God is not loving, just, or all-powerful?

God's ways are not our ways. We judge by earthly standards, seeing only the short-term, while God has a much larger plan in mind. He makes the sun to shine and the rain to fall on the just and the unjust alike. By our standards, there is no "justice" in this world. And maybe that's a good thing.

If we all got what we truly deserved, Shakespeare once observed, who among us would escape whipping?

"...*All* have sinned," Paul reminds us, "and fall short of the glory of God; they are now justified by his grace as a gift, through the redemption that is in Christ Jesus" (Rom 3:23–24, emphasis mine).

We say we want justice, but all have sinned. We don't need justice; we need mercy. Just as we did nothing to earn the great gift of life, we can never merit God's forgiveness. However, we can open ourselves to his saving grace by asking for forgiveness and by forgiving others.

We must leave our gifts at the altar and be reconciled with the brother we've wronged (cf. Mt 5:24). We must forgive the one who has wronged us, not seven times only but seventy times seven, with our actions and in our hearts, so that we may rid ourselves of hatred and bitterness and walk blameless in God's sight.

Why me, Lord?

When life seems to turn on us, we may feel that we could not possibly deserve such hardship. If we can't find anyone else to blame, we blame God. How can we reconcile God's love for us with the pain and suffering he sometimes seems to inflict on us?

Philosophy and theology have tried to explain the existence of evil in the world. There could be no good without evil, some say. Just as we couldn't know pleasure if we never experienced pain, or joy if we never felt sorrow, we couldn't know good except in contrast to bad.

Perhaps our suffering is purposeful, others suggest. Through suffering, we become able to understand and empathize with the sufferings of others and to react with compassion rather than judgment.

Both are no doubt true, but neither offers much comfort when you're hurting.

Almost twenty years ago, my wife was diagnosed with cancer and told she must undergo surgery immediately. Ellen handled the news with faith and courage, learning all she could about the disease and taking responsibility for her treatment. Through her strength, I held up fairly well—until the moment they wheeled her onto the elevator to take her to the operating room. As the doors closed behind her, my legs seemed to dissolve, and I literally staggered. Pain lanced my chest, hot tears stung my eyes. Raw fear and grief tore through my faith.

Ellen came through the surgery beautifully and faced her convalescence resolutely, more concerned for me and for our son than for herself. They got her out of bed and walking as soon as she could tolerate it. I walked her down the hall and back, going a little bit farther each time.

It was a real milestone when she could walk to the next ward, which happened to be the maternity ward. As I looked through the window at the babies in their bassinets, I began to weep and couldn't stop. Ellen tried to console me (Hey! Wasn't I supposed to be cheering *her* up?!) as sorrow and rage overwhelmed me.

Life seemed so unfair! Ellen had been a caring, loving Christian. She had devoted her life to helping others and seeking God. What kind of a loving, just God would give a person like that cancer? Perhaps he had simply washed his celestial hands of such matters and left Ellen to suffer from an unlucky toss of the genetic dice.

More than anything else in life, we had wanted another child after our son was born. Others got the children; she got cancer. Some don't even want the children they're given! Where's the justice in that?

Ellen has been cancer-free ever since (thank God!). Ultimately, our suffering deepened our faith and strengthened our marriage. I hope it made us more compassionate, more loving, more empathetic Christians. But at the time it just hurt—hurt so much, in fact, I wasn't sure I'd be able to bear it.

Is it fair that Ellen got cancer? No! My soul rages against the notion that she somehow deserved her disease. But is it any more fair that she recovered while cancer killed our friend Denise, a loving Christian who left behind a grieving husband and two small children? No. That's not fair, either.

It makes as much sense to ask "Why me?" in the good times as in the bad.

Is it fair that I was born in a country blessed with freedom and abundant resources; that I had loving, devoted parents; that I have a loving wife and son, live in a nice home, have plenty to eat and rewarding work to do? Did I somehow deserve to be born into my life instead of the lives of some of my students, who were born into poverty, abuse, and deprivation?

I don't remember passing some sort of qualifying test.

Is it fair that Christ had to die on the cross for my sins?

In the Old Testament, Job dares to question the fairness of a God who would rain down disaster on his good and faithful servant. Shouldn't the wicked, not the righteous, get the boils and plagues? When at last he is allowed to confront God with his outrage, God answers Job's questions with a bigger question: "Where were you when I laid the foundation of the earth?" (Job 38:4)

> "Have you commanded the morning since your days began,
>   and caused the dawn to know its place,

so that it might take hold of the skirts of the earth,
and the wicked be shaken out of it?...
Have you entered into the springs of the sea,
or walked in the recesses of the deep?
Have the gates of death been revealed to you,
or have you seen the gates of deep darkness?"
(38:12–13, 16–17)

Like Job, I wasn't present at creation, didn't get to glance at God's blueprints, was not privy to his reasoning when he set humanity in motion.

God's ways are not our ways. We cannot understand his plan. We see only a tiny part of his creation. We are stuck in space and time, trapped in our frail bodies, limited in our ability to perceive and process experience.

God is timeless and infinite. God sees what we cannot—that our time on earth is but a brief moment in our spiritual journeys.

From the world's perspective, life doesn't make sense. It isn't fair. It's not fair in the bad times, when we question God's love, and it's not fair in the good times, when God's special favor seems to have been poured out for us.

We must pray for God's guidance and open our souls to his Spirit to sustain us through all times. We must strive to live by God's precepts. We must ask God for a keen awareness of our sins, so that we can turn away from them and allow God to cleanse us and bring us closer to perfection.

When we do this, God will deliver us from all anxieties, in good times and in bad, and we'll leave judgment to him.

"I am an old man and have known a great many
troubles, but most of them never happened."

— MARK TWAIN

CHAPTER 17

Accepting the Inevitable

Worry can strip you of your defenses against disease, rob you
of your rest, and steal your serenity, your peace, and your joy.

God doesn't want us to worry. He told us so.

"Can any of you by worrying add a single hour to your span
of life?" (Mt 6:27).

"The LORD will keep you from all evil; he will keep your
life. The LORD will keep your going out and your coming in
from this time on and forevermore" (Ps 121:7–8).

You probably know the serenity prayer. Perhaps you even
incorporate it into your daily prayers.

> God grant me the serenity
> to accept the things I cannot change,
> the courage to change the things I can,
> and the wisdom to know the difference.

Learning what is and what isn't within your control is the
first step. Then you must accept those things you cannot
control.

I learned a lot about acceptance from an old Schnauzer named Hilda. (I could probably write a book entitled *Everything I Need to Know I Learned from My Dogs*.) After Dad died, Mom adopted Hilda, who was already well past middle age, from her hairdresser, and they looked after each other as best they could.

When Mom moved from California to Wisconsin to be near my wife and me, she naturally brought Hilda with her. (I say "naturally" because in my family, when we make a commitment to an animal, it's until death do us part.)

I remember grabbing the pet carrier as it thudded onto the luggage carousel at the Dane County Airport and lugging Hilda outside for her first sniff of Wisconsin air. When I opened the cage door, I encountered the most woeful-looking creature I've ever seen. Poor Hilda had fouled herself, and she was shaking with fear. Her legs wobbled so much, she could barely support herself as she stumbled out and took her first tentative steps into her new life. She had some sort of discharge from her eyes, and hunks of her fur had fallen out.

I reached out a hand to her. She looked at me through watery, bewildered eyes, perhaps remembering me from when I had visited, and licked my fingers. Then she looked around and heaved a sigh, as if to say, "Okay. What do I do now?"

She lived in the moment every day, even as advancing age left her increasingly unsteady and unsure. She simply did her best with what remained to her, enjoyed her food, kept us good company, and rolled on a patch of dirt in the yard when the sun shone.

Impressed by Hilda's great heart, Ellen and I have shared our lives with three more miniature Schnauzers (so far), and each has seemed to possess that great gift of making the best of things. Our newest family member is a rescue dog named Packer, whom we rechristened Pixie; she immediately claimed her place in our home and our hearts.

Although I've been greatly inspired by dogs, I've met people, too, who embodied courage and acceptance.

When we had to move Mom into a nursing home, I met many remarkable individuals, both among residents and staff. Prime among them was a woman named Olga. I soon learned that age, blindness, and the ravages of multiple diseases and operations had not conquered her indomitable spirit or slaked her genuine joy of living.

When she went to the hospital for what turned out to be her last surgery, the doctor warned her that she might not survive.

"Well, don't be so sad about it," Olga assured him. "Either I'll live and have more time with my grandchildren, or I'll die and be with my Jesus."

Olga figured she was a winner either way.

I met another winner, Chuck Wheeler, in the weight room of the community college where I taught in northern California. A vigorous man in his mid thirties, Chuck was lying on his back, preparing to bench press an enormous amount of weight. He had the thick muscles and sharp definition of a dedicated body builder. He wore dark glasses, even inside the gym, and his T-shirt carried the inscription, "Here comes Old Deadeye." He propped his white cane against the Universal machine while he went through his repetitions.

Old Deadeye could lift a lot more weight than I could!

Chuck appeared at my office door a few days later. He was writing a book, he told me, and he hoped I'd be willing to help him. I invited him in, and he told me his story.

A few years back, he explained, he'd been in a boating accident. As he and his friends were returning to the pier in Vallejo one night, the skipper, who had been drinking, mistook a light from a house up the hill for the dock light. Thinking the dock was still far off, he gunned the engine and rammed the boat into the pier. Chuck's two friends died, and he was blinded.

He endured a long, difficult convalescence, during which his wife divorced him. Excruciating headaches plagued him as he tried to adjust to his new life of darkness. He nearly went insane with rage, he said, at the injustice of what had happened to him.

He was writing about his experiences, and he wondered if I'd be willing to take a look at the first part of his manuscript. I was more than willing.

As he finished his story, which he told simply and without a trace of self-pity, one of my creative writing students appeared in the doorway, saw that I was busy, and started to leave.

"Come on in, Cindy," Chuck said before I had acknowledged her presence. "We're not telling any secrets."

Chuck got up, put a sheaf of papers on my desk, flashed a killer smile at Cindy, and left. Cindy took his place in the chair across the desk from me.

"How did he know it was you?" I asked her.

"The first time he did that, I thought it was my perfume," she explained. "But he does it even when I'm not wearing any scent. He says he can recognize my footsteps."

Poor Chuck and his "handicap," huh?

Chuck and I met often to discuss the story that was turning into a book; it was well written but needed revision—the story of every writer's life. The biggest problem he was having involved knowing when he had reached the bottom of the page. (This was before the word-processor, let alone voice recognition software.) We solved this problem with a simple attachment for his typewriter.

As I got to know him, I learned that going to school, bodybuilding, and writing a book weren't Chuck's only pastimes. He had custody of his nine-year-old son, and together they were building an addition on his house.

Chuck eventually moved to Oregon and I to Wisconsin. Years passed, but I never forgot him. One Sunday morning I was enjoying the book supplement to *The New York Times* and became engrossed in a review of a novel called *Snakewalk,* which involved a man blinded in a boating accident who…Wait a minute! Quickly I checked the author's name. Chuck Wheeler! He had written his book, found a major publisher for it, and secured a review in the Sunday *Times*!

A clear case of the student surpassing the teacher—and a vivid example of accepting the conditions of your life and making the most of them. "Not my will but yours be done."

In the Scriptures, when Shadrach, Meshach, and Abednego refused to worship the golden idol, an enraged King Nebuchadnezzar had them cast into the fiery furnace (Dan 3:19–29). The three men pledged to follow the God of their fathers even if he chose not to save them from death. They didn't bargain with God ("I'll believe in you if you save me"). Their faith didn't depend on circumstances. They were ready to accept God's will, whether in painful death or miraculous salvation, with equal faith.

Mary, the mother of Jesus, didn't bargain with God either. In the first chapter of Luke's Gospel, we read that she was "much perplexed" by the appearance of an angel, who told her she would conceive and bear a son who would reign over the house of Jacob forever.

She didn't question or argue. She didn't ask for guarantees. She simply said, "Here I am, the servant of the Lord; let it be with me according to your word" (Lk 1:38).

When Jesus himself prayed in the Garden of Gethsemane the night the soldiers came for him, he felt "grieved and agitated" (cf. Mt 26:37). He asked the Father, "If it is possible, let this cup pass from me." But with his next breath, he said, "Yet not what I want but what you want."

He had to endure the additional sorrow of finding his friends asleep, unable to keep watch with him as the trial of the cross drew near. Yet twice more he prayed, "My Father, if this cannot pass unless I drink it, your will be done."

Jesus accepted the Father's will for him, however terrifying the consequences.

Through experience, prayer, worship, and Scripture study, you learn to discern God's will for you. In him you find the courage to confront the things you can change and to accept the things you cannot change. With this faith and acceptance comes the peace that surpasses all human understanding, the peace God alone can provide.

"Do not worry about tomorrow; tomorrow will take care of itself" (cf. Mt 6:34).

"Come to me, all you that are weary and are carrying heavy burdens, and I will give you rest. Take my yoke upon you, and learn from me; for I am gentle and humble in heart, and you will find rest for your souls. For my yoke is easy, and my burden is light."

—MATTHEW 11:28–30

CHAPTER 18

Surrendering to Fear and Faith

Struggling with her faith, a friend of mine sought the help of a spiritual counselor. When she continually resisted his advice, he told her, "Your ego doesn't like letting go of the idea that you're the center of the universe."

She stayed stuck in spiritual crisis for months, "feeling my faithlessness, taking it in silence, feeling it fully." She called it "a terrible and perhaps necessary journey."

My friend later explained. "It is only when life begins to emerge from the void," she said, "that one knows the fertility of that void. Faith and angst go together. How could we go through something like that without anxiety? How could such an endeavor be without pain? It hurts to let go of what we think we are."

Faith, she concluded, is "beyond description. It just is."

I have felt the anguish of uncertainty and despair. I'm sure you have, too. "I can't go on," the soul says. "I give up."

But life doesn't let you give up, and you must go on.

Somehow in those painful moments of complete surrender, I've felt a peace I can't explain. Nothing in my circumstances had changed. Whatever was bothering me before remained. The universe still seemed indifferent to my pain. But I felt God's presence in the midst of it.

In such moments, I believe we experience a kind of death and rebirth. The "I" that insists on placing itself at the center of creation and being in charge dies in this moment. We sense the stirrings of the Spirit that God places within each of us. Faith is reborn.

It's frightening. New realities, new possibilities, always are. But when I surrender to the fear, I can feel the exhilaration of walking with Christ.

Our culture encourages us to run away from such intense inner experience. This is a great mistake. Without the death and resurrection of faith, we'll never grow in the Spirit. Fear isn't the enemy. It's a sign that wonderful things are about to happen, are happening, within us.

Stand still. Feel all your fear. Embrace it.

Many years ago, I stood in the carport of my brother's apartment in Phoenix and watched lightning fill the night sky. I had never seen such raw energy. Much later, after Ellen and I moved to Wisconsin, I watched the downspout of a tornado twist and snap our backyard maple tree as if it were no more substantial than a blade of grass. (Yes, I should have been in the basement. And no, I don't stand at the window watching tornadoes any more.)

Such experiences are at once terrifying and exhilarating.

For me, the experience of letting fear flood me feels like that. No wonder I spent so much of my life trying to evade it!

Now I surrender to the storm. In its own time it passes, leaving behind a calm much deeper than anything I've ever experienced. I felt it when my father died and again when I lost my mother. It was their final gift to me.

I have survived and am unharmed. Now what should I fear?

"Darkness is not dark for you, and night shines as the day. Darkness and light are but one" (Ps 139:12).

Now at last I can embrace the paradox of fear/faith. I can trust God, who is present in everything and everyone. I can begin to live the central paradox of our shared faith: "For whoever wishes to save his life will lose it, but whoever loses his life for my sake will find it" (Mt 16:25).

When you let your fear flow out of you and are reborn in faith, you can claim the promise of Sacred Scripture: "With the LORD on my side I do not fear. What can mortals do to me?" (Ps 118:6)

Keep in your heart the promise Jesus gave to the disciples before he ascended into heaven: "I am with you always, to the end of the age" (Mt 28:20).

And remember always the beautiful words of Julian of Norwich: "All will be well, and all will be well, and all will be very well."

MARSHALL J. COOK is a professor in the Department of Liberal Studies and the Arts at the University of Wisconsin-Madison. He teaches workshops, seminars, and credit courses on writing and editing, creativity, stress management, and media relations, and he often speaks at conferences nationwide.

Marshall edits *Creativity Connection, the Writer's Quarterly Encouragement*, a newsletter for writers and independent publishers. He has authored twenty-five books and hundreds of magazine articles.

Marshall holds his BA in creative writing and his MA in communications from Stanford University. He has been married to Ellen since 1968, and they have one son, Jeremiah. When not writing or teaching, Marshall likes to read, jog, lift weights, and talk back to the television (not all at the same time). He is a passionate minor league baseball fan, drives the back roads, and eats in small town cafes.

BOOKS & MEDIA

The Daughters of St. Paul operate book and media centers at the following addresses. Visit, call or write the one nearest you today, or find us on the World Wide Web, www.pauline.org

CALIFORNIA
3908 Sepulveda Blvd, Culver City, CA 90230	310-397-8676
2460 Broadway Street, Redwood City, CA 94063	650-369-4230
5945 Balboa Avenue, San Diego, CA 92111	858-565-9181

FLORIDA
145 S.W. 107th Avenue, Miami, FL 33174	305-559-6715

HAWAII
1143 Bishop Street, Honolulu, HI 96813	808-521-2731
Neighbor Islands call:	866-521-2731

ILLINOIS
172 North Michigan Avenue, Chicago, IL 60601	312-346-4228

LOUISIANA
4403 Veterans Memorial Blvd, Metairie, LA 70006	504-887-7631

MASSACHUSETTS
885 Providence Hwy, Dedham, MA 02026	781-326-5385

MISSOURI
9804 Watson Road, St. Louis, MO 63126	314-965-3512

NEW JERSEY
561 U.S. Route 1, Wick Plaza, Edison, NJ 08817	732-572-1200

NEW YORK
150 East 52nd Street, New York, NY 10022	212-754-1110

PENNSYLVANIA
9171-A Roosevelt Blvd, Philadelphia, PA 19114	215-676-9494

SOUTH CAROLINA
243 King Street, Charleston, SC 29401	843-577-0175

TENNESSEE
4811 Poplar Avenue, Memphis, TN 38117	901-761-2987

TEXAS
114 Main Plaza, San Antonio, TX 78205	210-224-8101

VIRGINIA
1025 King Street, Alexandria, VA 22314	703-549-3806

CANADA
3022 Dufferin Street, Toronto, ON M6B 3T5	416-781-9131

¡También somos su fuente para libros,
videos y música en español!